Victorian Terraced Houses in Lancaster

by

Andrew White and Michael Winstanley

Centre for North-West Regional Studies
University of Lancaster
1996

Victorian Terraced Houses in Lancaster
by Andrew White and Michael Winstanley

This volume is the thirty-third in a series published by the Centre for North-West Regional Studies at the University of Lancaster. Details of titles which are still available may be obtained from the Centre.

Editorial Board
Elizabeth Roberts, David Shotter, Angus Winchester

ISSN 0308–4310

Published by the Centre for North-West Regional Studies,
University of Lancaster, 1996

Copyright © University of Lancaster, 1996
Text copyright © Andrew White and Michael Winstanley, 1996

Typeset and originated by Carnegie Publishing Ltd,
18 Maynard St, Preston, Lancs.
Printed and bound in the UK by The Alden Press, Oxford

British Library Cataloguing in Publication Data
A CIP record for this book is available from the British Library

ISBN 0-901800-96-1

All rights reserved
No part of this publication may be reproduced, stored in a retrieval system, or transmitted in any form or by any means mechanical, electronic, photocopying or otherwise, without the prior permission of the publisher.

Contents

Acknowledgements iv

Introduction: the Victorian Terrace 1

1. **Building Lancaster** 7
   Building Developments 7
   Larger Developments 8
   House Types 15
   Domestic Services 17
   Building Materials 20
   Building and Planning Control 23

2. **Builders and Backers** 25
   Employers as Builders of Housing 25
   The Builders 26
   Raising Finance 30
   Built by the Pharaohs 31

3. **The Terraces' Owners** 35
   Landlords 35
   Owner-Occupiers 40

4. **Servicing the Suburbs** 43
   Shops and Street Traders 43
   Lodgings, Pubs and Off-licences 49
   Churches and Schools 51

Epilogue **The Edwardian Era and After** 55

Gazetteer 57
   Lancaster (including Bulk and Scotforth townships) 57
   Skerton 72

Primary Sources and Select Bibliography 75

Acknowledgements

The authors would like to thank the many people who helped in the research and production of this book; at Lancaster City Museums Susan Ashworth, Paul Thompson and Andy Hornby; at Lancaster University Dr. Elizabeth Roberts, Dr Colin Pooley and Professor John Walton; at the University College of S. Martin James Price and former staff member Geoff Boulton; at Lancaster Central Library Alan Duckworth and his staff; and at the Lancashire Record Office all the staff who fetched and carried rate books and building applications from the stores. We would also like to thank George and Margaret Niven for useful information on Williamsons and Mr R. Stuart, and Mr and Mrs F. W. Swarbrick for access to their property deeds. Finally, staff at Bairstow Eves, Reeds Rains and Cornerstone estate agents were most helpful in allowing access to empty and relatively unaltered houses which were on their books at the time, while Lancaster City Council Legal Services provided access to the splendid series of property deeds in their possession.

This book began life as the research for an exhibition at Lancaster City Museum in 1996 entitled 'On the Street where you Live'. The first author (AW), intrigued by the loose ends left at the end of researching the building of Georgian Lancaster, began work on the task and quickly called upon the second author (MW) for his already voluminous knowledge of shops and services as well as the economic background. The collaboration is roughly this; Introduction and Epilogue by MW; Chapters I and 2, principally AW, but 'Built by the Pharaohs' by MW; Chapters 3 and 4, principally MW ; Gazetteer, principally by AW but with additions by MW. In addition both authors have read and criticised each other's sections, and many of the comments have been incorporated in this text.

All illustrations, unless otherwise credited, are by the authors.

Introduction: the Victorian Terrace

The centre of Lancaster as we know it today still owes much to the Georgian age.[1] Over a hundred buildings from this period survive, including many of the most prominent ones. However, during the nineteenth century the urban landscape was dramatically transformed as the old town was gradually surrounded on all sides by new terraces, inhabited by all social classes except the very richest and poorest.

Until the 1840s residential development hardly existed outside the medieval street-pattern, apart from some peripheral growth to the east, in the area around Dalton Square, Marton Street, Rosemary Lane, and St Leonardgate. Like the town centre itself, this district was characterised by a contrasting combination of fine houses, business premises, teeming yards, cramped courts and back-to-back housing, much of which has now been demolished. Only the exceptionally rich and privileged had been able to escape from the town, as the large detached residences in their own grounds just beyond the borough boundaries testified.

By the end of the century houses had been erected on land all around the town, many of them in the grounds of these outlying mansions. To the south the new terraces straddled the main road leading to the village of Scotforth. On the hills to the east and south-east whole new estates – Dry Dock, Freehold, Primrose, Moorlands, Bowerham – were laid out. To the west tentacles of growth took in the edges of the Marsh. To the north the river Lune formed a natural and long-established boundary but Skerton, previously an independent village, partook of the same growth and ultimately became Lancaster's northern suburb. Unlike the mixed quarters of the old town, these new streets were almost exclusively residential with only a sprinkling of shops to service the daily needs of their inhabitants.

This transition occurred gradually. The first streets to emerge, just to the east of the town, initially had courts and back-to-backs, and they were not purely residential, containing a variety of commercial premises, stabling and building yards. The covenants attached to the Freehold development in the 1850s, however, were symptomatic of what was to come. These restricted the erection of any buildings specifically adapted for business or trade to certain plots on the estate and forbade any 'noisy, noxious, dangerous or offensive' activities.[2] Although the Marsh and Dry Dock estates of the 1870s were adjacent to, and built primarily to house the workers for, James Williamson's and the Storeys' nearby textile mills, they also contained no industrial or commercial premises, other than shops. Thereafter, as building extended on to what had previously been green-field sites on the outskirts, housing estates became precisely that – socially segregated, residential dormitories whose inhabitants relied on income generated from employment or business elsewhere in the town.

The timing of this housing development was directly related to the fluctuating prosperity of the local economy. In the 1850s and 1860s, low levels of building activity reflected the depressed state of the town's trade, but there was a sustained boom in the last thirty years of the nineteenth century, especially in the 1870s and 1890s, as the major employers, including James Williamson, the Storey brothers and the Lancaster Wagon Company, all dramatically expanded their operations.[3] The chronology of housing provision, therefore, was rather different from that of Lancashire's early textile towns but it closely mirrored national

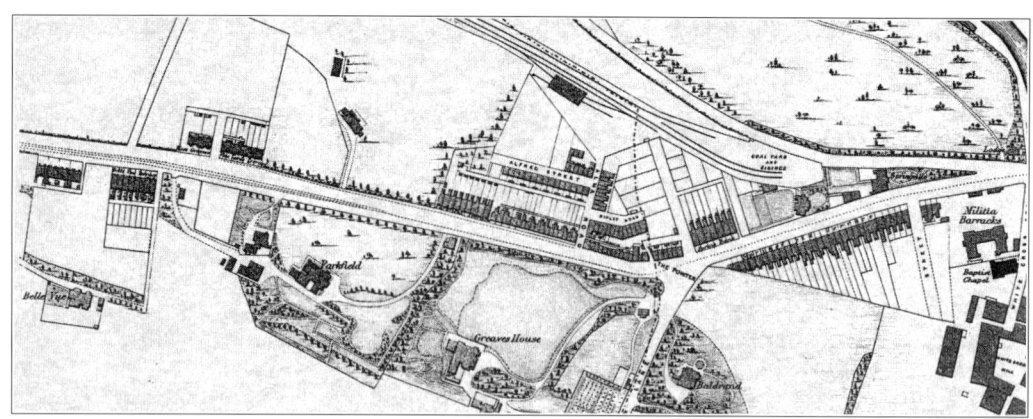

Detail from Harrison & Hall's map of Lancaster, 1877, showing the detached residences in their wooded grounds, the ribbon development of substantial properties with long rear gardens along South Road and Greaves Road, and the streets of smaller terraces which grew up behind them.

A panoramic view of the same area, looking south from the top of Storeys' chimney on a summer's evening in the early 1900s. Meadowside, visible in the foreground, had recently been built on land owned by Thomas Barrow of Baldrand, the large house on the left. Despite the concentration of properties to the east of the main road, the overwhelming impression is still rural. (Lancaster City Museums)

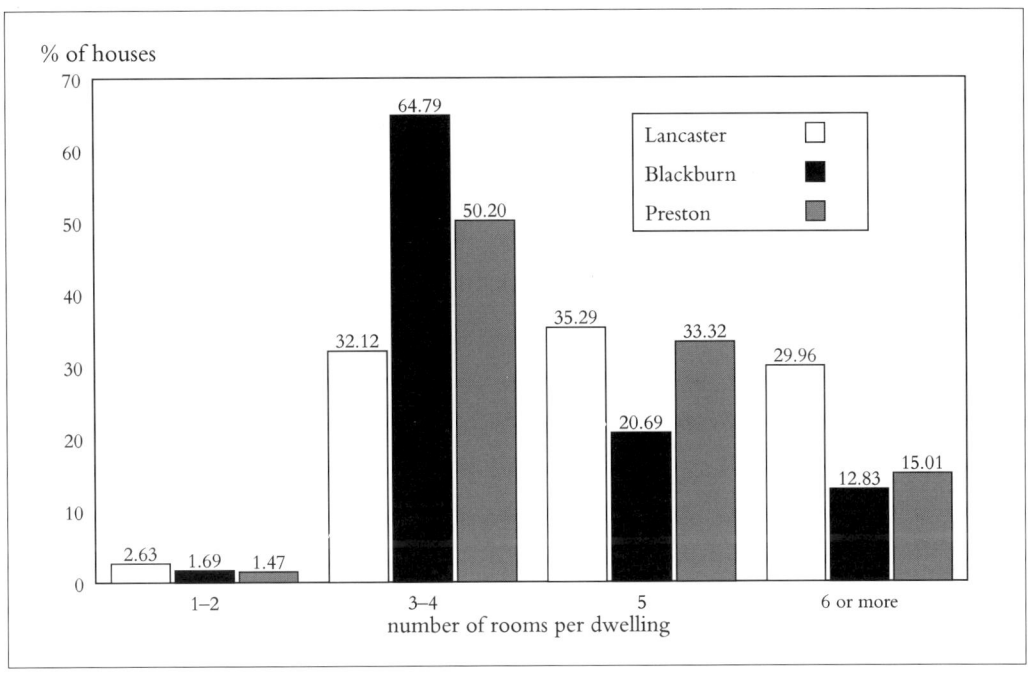

Housing profile of Lancaster, Blackburn and Preston, 1911. Source: Census Tables for Lancashire, 1911.

cycles of building activity in the half century before 1914.[4] This is hardly surprising, since the demand for the products of its major firms – floor coverings, oil cloth and window blinds – was largely determined by the buoyancy of the national housing market.[5] When housebuilding slumped dramatically in the Edwardian era, Lancaster's industrial and residential expansion also came to a shuddering halt, leaving a legacy of half-finished streets which were only gradually extended and filled in over the next half century.

The physical nature of the houses which were built reflected the changing social structure of the town and the wealth, income and status of their inhabitants. Each phase of development represented not just the architectural fashion of the time, but the fine status-distinctions which characterised Victorian society. Tradesmen, professionals, white collar employees and workers respectively clustered into streets and districts which were physically, and possibly socially and culturally, separate. The layout of the streets was such that inhabitants of middle-class areas did not have to pass through the poorer streets on their way into the centre. They also rarely had to endure the worst of the smoke and industrial pollution, since few were downwind of the town centre or the larger manufacturing establishments.

The smallest terraces built mainly between the 1870s and 1900 had just four rooms – two-up, two-down – but there was a relatively high proportion of five- and six-roomed properties which had either an extra storey, or a back scullery with extra bedroom over it. Some houses were embellished with a bay window or small front garden to distance them from the public thoroughfare, and were intended to appeal to town's numerous white-collar employees, while there continued to be a demand for rather grander residences from the prosperous business and professional classes. All this meant that the Lancaster's housing profile was very different from the cotton towns of south-east Lancashire.

During the 1950s and 1960s a wholesale demolition of older terraces was undertaken in many British towns. Lancaster did not totally

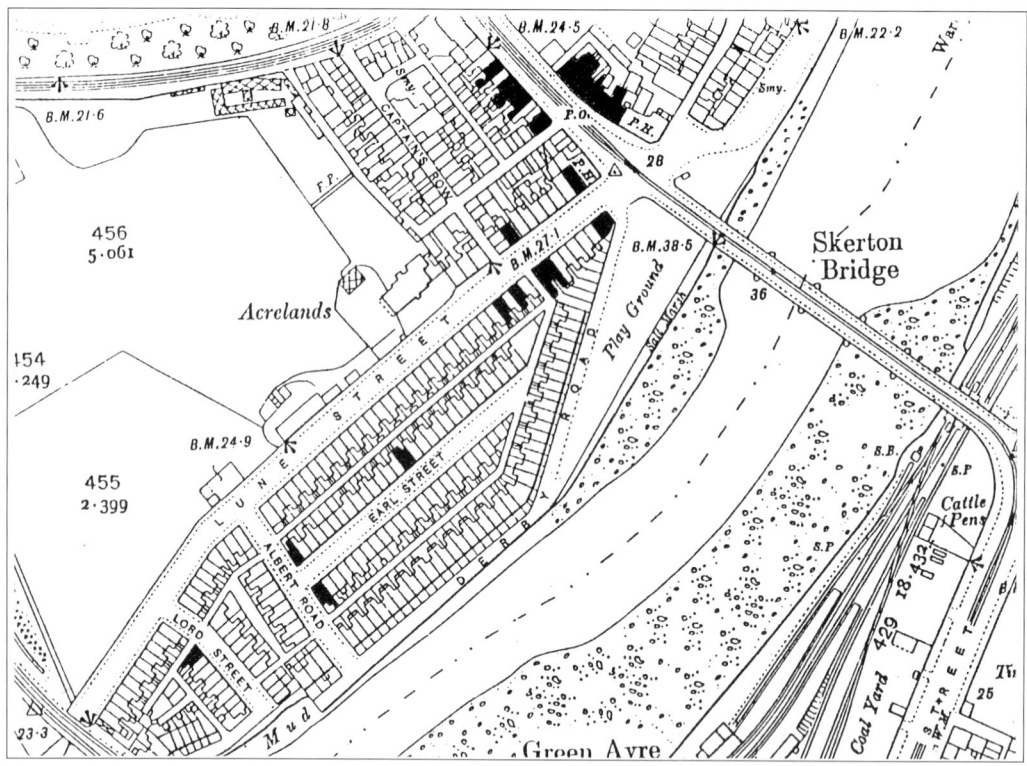

Part of Skerton from the O.S. 25″ map of 1913. The contrast between the ordered terraces built around 1880 and the older, jumbled warren off Captain's Row (now demolished), is clearly evident. Shading has been added to indicate the location of retail premises in the area. Note the concentration on Owen Road and the strategic positioning of others in the new estate (see Chapter 4).

escape this. During the 1920s and 1930s, many of its central courts and yards were pulled down, while some more substantial terraced properties to the east of the town centre were flattened in the 1960s and 1970s to make way for a relief road which has yet to be, and may never be, built, and some properties to the south of the town were victims of a road widening scheme in the 1970s. Fortunately, however, the vast majority of its Victorian terraces have survived. To some extent this can be attributed to the relative lack of pressure for substantial commercial and retail redevelopment during the 1960s, and then to the subsequent reaction against the style of architecture which characterised those decades. It is also the case, however, that a high proportion of the town's older residential property is 'solid in the extreme', having been built in stone, and erected in conformity with increasingly stringent local authority regulations from the 1850s.[6] Not surprisingly, a century after they were built, Lancaster's stone terraces retain much of their appeal, both to live in and to appreciate as an integral part of the architectural heritage.

In this book we explore the origins, development and significance of these Victorian terraces. We deal with what the houses were, and are, like; who built them and in what order; what they were like to live in; who owned them; and how services like shops, schools, pubs and churches were provided to service their residents. In doing so we hope to show that their development represented more than a mere tran-

A view down Lord Street, Skerton, from Lune Street looking towards the river around the turn of the century. The corner shop on the right and some cottages adjacent to the river have been demolished. Note the unmade road and the apology for street lighting. The viaduct carrying the railway to Morecambe is visible in the background. (Lancaster Central Library)

sition in architectural design; it was associated with new sources of financing and a restructuring of the building industry. These changes were also accompanied by a new pattern of property ownership. On the one hand there was an increasing tendency for the minority who could afford to do so to become owner-occupiers. Meanwhile, however, although most houses continued to owned by landlords with just few properties each, often in the immediate vicinity of their own residences, several individuals, usually connected in some way with the building trades, emerged as substantial owners of the newer, smaller terraces. Above all, as the estates matured and specialist services developed to cater for the physical, educational and spiritual needs of their residents, a distinctive way of life emerged, the essentials of which have persisted well into the late twentieth century.

Notes

1. S. H. Penney, *Lancaster: the Evolution of its Townscape* (1981); A. White, *The Buildings of Georgian Lancaster* (1992).
2. Freehold Estate Building Regulations, 1853, Lancaster Central Library, MS 6566.
3. M. Winstanley, 'The Town Transformed, 1815–1914', in A. White (ed.), *A History of Lancaster, 1193–1993* (1993), 145–98.
4. S. B. Saul, 'House Building in England, 1890–1914', *Economic History Review*, 15 (1962–63), 119–26; R. Rodger, *Housing in Urban Britain, 1780–1914* (1995).
5. P. J. Gooderson, *Lord Linoleum: Lord Ashton, Lancaster and the Rise of the British Oilcloth and Linoleum Industry* (1996), 110–16.
6. J. B. Cullingworth, *Housing in Transition: a case study in the City of Lancaster, 1958–62* (1963), 20.

1

Building Lancaster

Building Developments

As we have seen in the introduction the move in Lancaster during the nineteenth century was for suburban development which called for increasing quantities of land on the fringes of the town, including former farmland and elements of large estates. Demand for building land on the outskirts of the town could not always be met. In the eighteenth century a large area of land to the east of the medieval core had belonged to the Dalton family and in 1784 John Dalton obtained a private Act of Parliament to break the entail on his estate, so as to allow the lease and eventual sale of this land for building.[1] Further to the south lay property of the Marton family, undeveloped during the eighteenth century, which was sold in a series of smaller lots by G. B. H. Marton in 1844.[2] The difference was that while the Dalton estate insisted on its property being developed to a coherent plan, with controls on the size and appearance of houses the Marton estate made no such rules. Buildings put up in George St, Marton St and Thurnham St were small and mean, crammed as tightly together as possible. Sixty years had made a great difference in Lancaster's fortunes; in 1784 there were gentlemen prepared to build themselves elegant town houses. By 1844 small entrepreneurs were starting to run up speculative rows of the cheapest houses they could build for the growing working classes.

This highlights the fact that before 1901 there was no coherent strategy for development control. Builders ran up housing wherever there was an opportunity. From the middle of the century there were bye-laws and health regulations and from about 1880 there were quite strong planning controls, but these were essentially reactive. The Plans Committee approved or turned down plans submitted to them, as they still do, but there was at the time no concept of 'planning brief' or 'structure plan' to ensure that development followed coherent lines and one element did not damage the prospects of another. Occasionally the Corporation would encourage building or rebuilding to a new building-line, in the interests of wider and more healthy streets, as at Moorgate, or at China Lane in the town centre, using its powers as a Sanitary Authority. In general the quality of a development depended upon any controls as to size, price and freedom from nuisance trades which the owner of a landed estate might wish to impose, and the likely rental value which buyers might receive from their properties. Its location depended very much upon what land was currently available for sale, not upon any policy of zoning for residential development.

Generally building was carried out field by field. A sort of 'domino effect' meant that building on one site automatically rendered neighbouring sites attractive. Sale of part of the Bowerham Estate to the War Office in 1874 to build the new Barracks must have stimulated further sales in that vicinity, leading to the building of the Adelphi Street/Golgotha Road area, and also to the streets of the Primrose area. The shape of building plots was often determined by field boundaries, themselves sometimes determined by medieval ploughmen! On Greaves Rd, however, the developments more often took the form of a roadside strip, the backland waiting until the twentieth century for housing to reach

Early pre-byelaw housing including back-to-backs in the George St/Marton St area, from St Peter's church spire, *c.* 1900. (Lancaster City Museums)

it. The difficulty in laying out housing in relatively small irregular patches meant that road junctions were often very awkward, while the need to maintain set standards of rear access lanes produced some difficult building plots. Plots at the corners of two streets were often larger than usual and were intended from the outset as shops. Builders often went to considerable lengths to provide equal-sized if oddly-shaped back yards where the street line and plot boundary converged. In general the larger the piece of land to be developed the more economically and fully could it be used. Much of the earlier development was small in scale, no more than a street or two at a time, but by the 1880s the scale was starting to increase.

Larger Developments

As we have seen, building took place wherever there was land available either on the fringes of the town or by infilling between existing houses. Some developments were larger, however, mainly because a pre-existing estate was for sale. A few examples are given below of some of these larger developments.

Freehold

The Freehold was Lancaster's earliest and largest building estate with the longest period of activity. Furthermore it was unlike any of the other estates, being established for political reasons rather than as a financial speculation. The story is told in detail elsewhere.[3] Briefly the project developed as part of a wider national movement which began in the 1840s with the aim of increasing the number of freeholders of land and hence widening the county franchise, since the right to vote was based upon the ownership of property worth two pounds or more annually. It was more particularly associated

The Freehold Estate, from Harrison & Hall's map, 1877.

with the Liberal interest. There had been earlier attempts to set up cheap freeholds in order to increase the Liberal vote in places like Kendal.[4] A piece of land covering 38 acres outside the existing built-up area was purchased in January 1852 for £6,500 and was parcelled out into 364 building lots by March 1853.[5] The plots were large, in order to qualify for the magical valuation of £2, and the distinctive feature of the estate, very long gardens, was alien to the concept of town houses at the time and not matched anywhere else in Lancaster. Because of the costs involved the plots took a long time to sell. Prime sites such as the corners went first, mainly to small capitalists. But the market for such property was limited and by the 1860s some of the plots had been subdivided while on others short terraces had been erected by speculators for rent, so that in 1861 there were 102 householders but only 30 actual owners.[6] The estate was largely unsuccessful as a piece of social engineering because there were not enough people in Lancaster able to buy outright, so consequently the building process was very long drawn-out. There are still gaps in the estate to this day.

Freehold was laid out on a grid. Three east-west roads, Borrowdale, Dalton and Rydal Roads, are crossed at right angles by Ulleswater, Grasmere, Windermere and Derwent Roads. Only the outer sides of Borrowdale and Rydal Roads have any houses on them, while Dalton Road has only the sides of houses and their long gardens in the cross streets. The very long gardens are mostly aligned east-west and there is considerable social stratification in the estate, the larger houses being uphill (to the east) and smaller ones downhill (to the west). It is not primarily an estate of terraces, most houses being detached or in pairs, but the lower part of the estate does show a variety of short terraces.

9

Dry Dock

The streets known as 'Dry Dock', named from the Dry Dock on the Lancaster Canal which lies immediately to the north west, were built on a piece of land originally known as 'Nuns' Fields'. Nun Street, Mill Street, Garnett Street and Wolseley Street were conceived in the late 1870s and built over a period of years. A plan of the site, offering 106 lots for houses on application to Mr G. L. Shaw, joiner and builder, or to Messrs Holden & Whelon, solicitors, is in the Central Library.[7] Garnett Street appears on Harrison & Hall's map of 1877. The site is a particularly awkward one, being hemmed in on three sides by the Lancaster Canal, Bath Mill and the pre-existing Freehold Estate. Some of the individual plots on the west side of Garnett Street or the east side of Wolseley Street are very constricted. Quick access to the town centre was provided by a foot bridge over the Lancaster Canal in 1882.

Marsh

Lune Road and Willow Lane, leading south from St George's Quay, gave access to new building ground to the west of the town, on the edges of the former marsh which gives its name to the area. To the north of West Road an area of land known as 'Briery Field' belonging to Mr H. R. Ford was sold in 1876–7 and acquired by several speculative builders including J. Kitchen and Pye Bros. who built Charnley Street, Briery Street, Ford Street, Marsh Street and Windmill Street, the latter close to the site of the Marsh Windmill, demolished soon afterwards. To the south of West Road another group of streets, Salisbury Road, Ashbrook Street, Meadow Street, Beech Street and Stanley Place, took shape in 1889–90. There is no very distinctive stylistic connection between these houses, which may have been put up by a number of speculators. The little group of houses fronting Willow Lane immediately to the south and

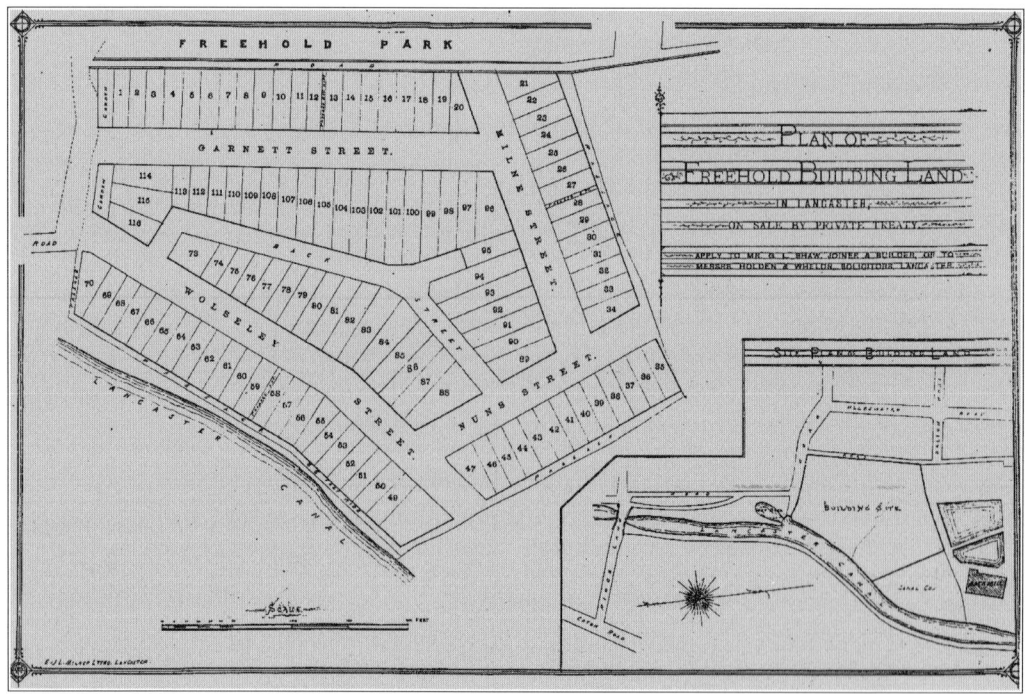

Plan of the Dry Dock estate, as set out for building in the late 1870s. (Lancaster Central Library)

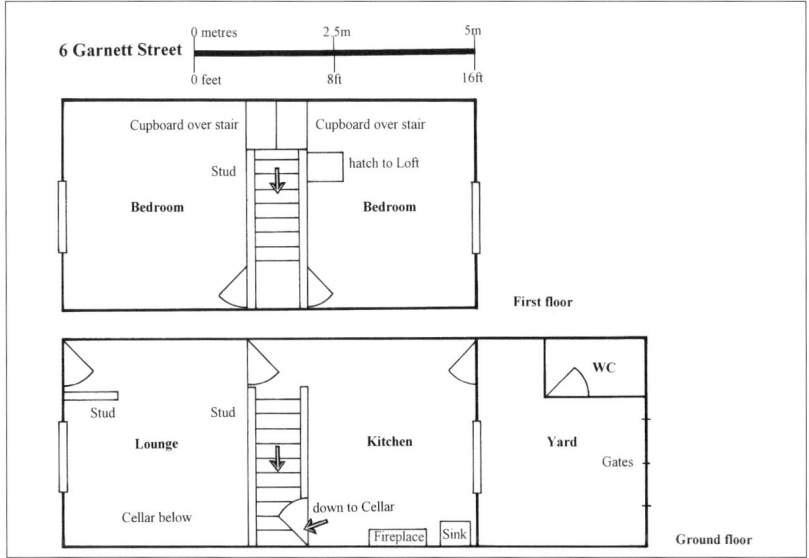

Plan of 6 Garnett Street, on the Dry Dock estate. (Drawn by Paul Thompson)

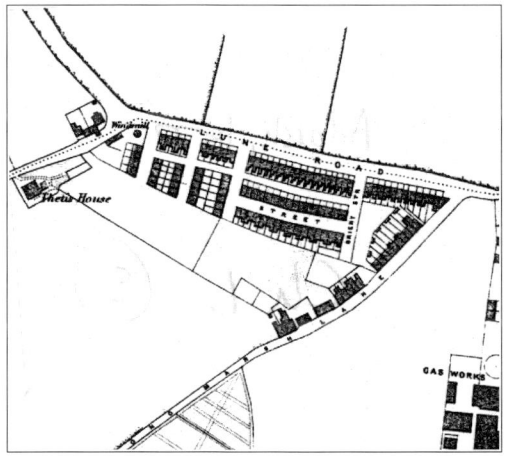

Building work in progress on the Marsh, from Harrison & Hall's map, 1877.

known as 'Willow Grove' seem to have been built a few years earlier, in 1886.

Woodville Gardens

Woodville Gardens had served as allotments for people living in nearby streets for many years. In 1882 the land was sold for building upon and the four streets, Woodville Street, Williamson Road, Melbourne Street and Greenfield Street were the result. This development lay below the earlier Freehold and had to fit in between it and Bath Mill, also accommodating the existing streets of Bath Street and Bath Mill Lane. The result is a rather awkward layout. The houses were largely occupied within four years.

Bulk

The four streets of Ridge Street, Green Street, Albion Street and Hinde Street, together with Gladstone Terrace which fronts onto the old Caton Road, all lay outside the borough boundary of Lancaster when they were built in the 1890s. The boundary lay along the little beck which now runs underground below Factory Hill. The consequence of this is that the borough bye-laws did not apply here, although the Lancaster Union had its own, rather less rigorous, set.

Primrose

Primrose occupies the site of a house and gardens known as 'Primrose Hill', from which it takes its name. It lies to the south-east of the town centre and a little to the south of Moorlands, which post-dates it. The lower part of the development lies upon the Bowerham Estate and plans for houses at the southern end of Dale Street and in The Grove had to be scrutinised

11

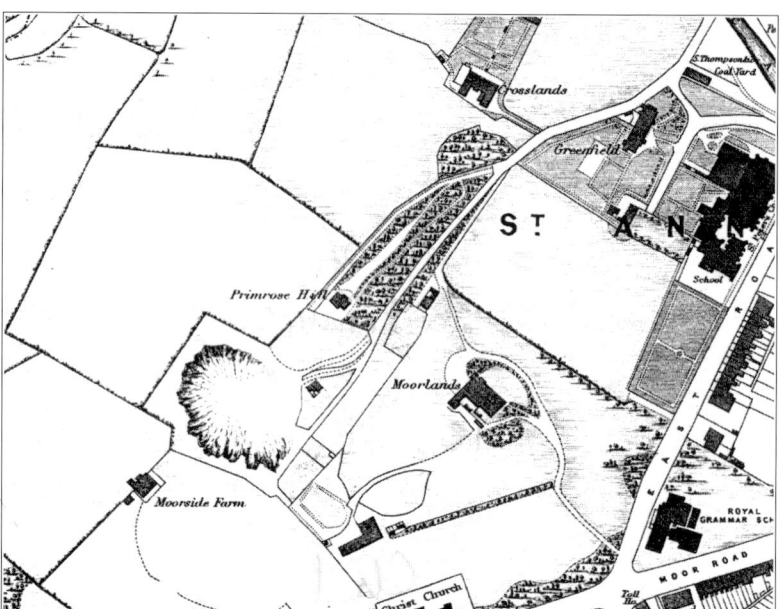

The large houses of Moorlands and Primrose Hill occupying the sites of the future Moorlands and Primrose estates, from Harrison & Hall's map, 1877.

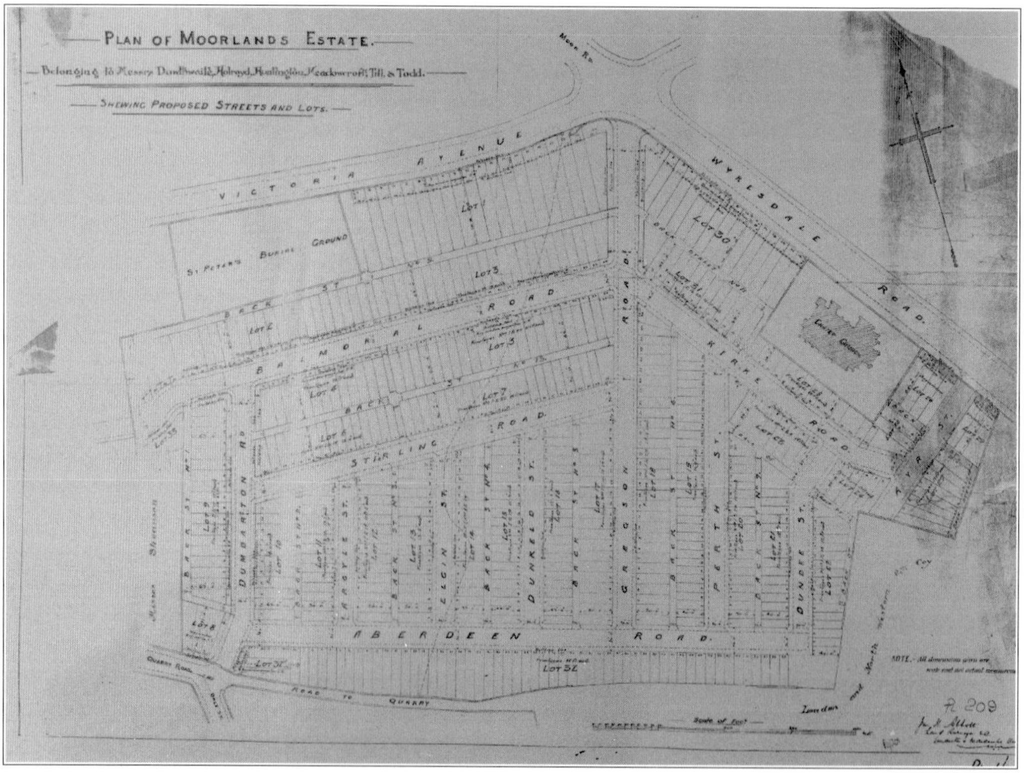

Plan of building land at Bowerham in the 1880s; development followed rather different lines in detail to create the present Adelphi St/Golgotha Rd area. (Lancaster Central Library)

View of Moorlands soon after building, from St Peter's church spire, *c.* 1900. (Lancaster Central Library)

first by the owners of Bowerham House.[8] Numerous builders took a hand in the building of Primrose, which is far less uniform in character than its later neighbour, Moorlands. In general the larger houses lie at the northern, eastern and southern sides, in Dale Street, Prospect Street, Primrose Street and St Oswald Street. Further up the hill most of the houses are of the most basic two storey flush-fronted types. The development consists of eleven streets. The earliest parts, Dale Street, Prospect Street and Primrose Street, got under way in the early 1880s, while the streets further up the hill are principally of the 1890s.

Moorlands

Moorlands House, the property of the Gregson family, lay to the east of the town centre and isolated from the tide of housing which had by the 1880s started to flow up the hill towards it. The house itself was insulated by its surrounding pleasure grounds and woodland. Following the death of Henry Gregson's widow, Anne Gregson, there was a court case in Chancery over the will[9] and subsequently the whole Moorlands estate, including the house, stables, outbuildings and gardens, was put up for auction in seventeen lots on 6th September 1893. It sold to a consortium of local builders for £15,000.[10] A series of detailed clauses outlined the number, size and value of houses to be erected upon the estate. A plan accompanying the catalogue shows the land laid out for streets and building lots but leaving an 'island' in the middle where the house itself would have survived, no doubt very uncomfortably hemmed in by its new neighbours.[11] The exact course of events is not clear but within a short time the whole development plan had been rethought. A plan in the Central Library[12] shows a wholly new layout in which the house has been

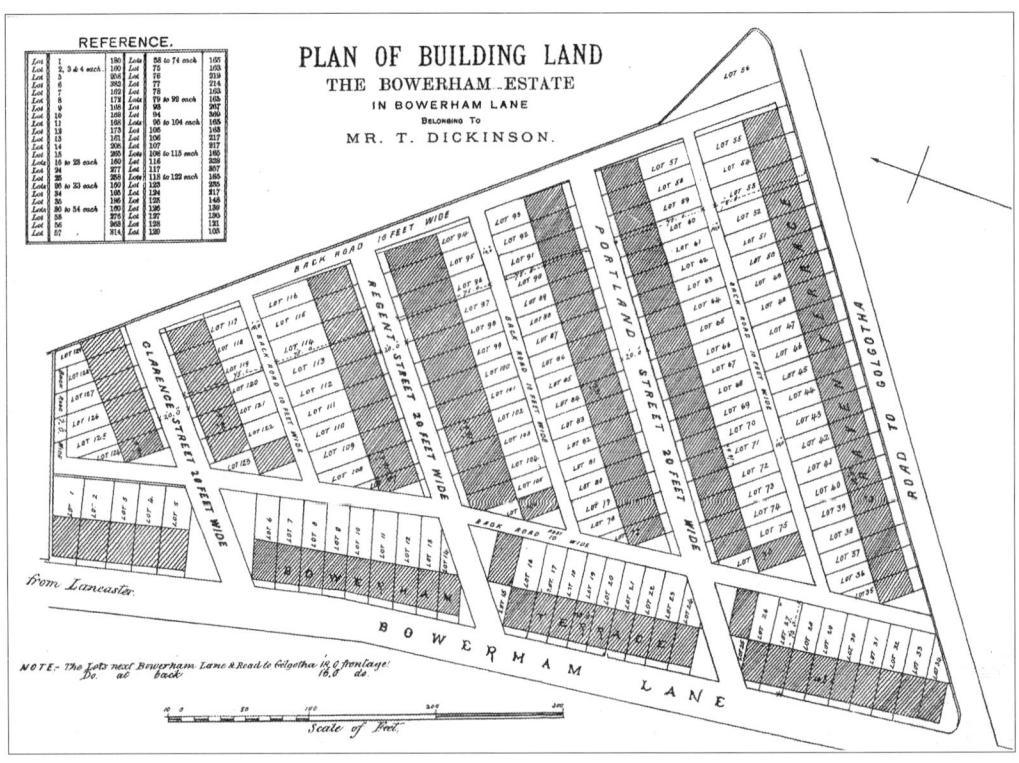

Plan of proposed layout of the Moorlands Estate, 1893. (Lancaster Central Library)

removed and the streets around it have been realigned accordingly, providing much more building land. The names of the new owners – Messrs Dowthwaite, Holroyd, Huntington, Meadowcroft, Till & Todd – appear in the top left hand corner of this plan and there are now thirty-two lots for building, each marked out with a series of individual house-plots. The group of builders named on the plan formed the 'Moorlands Estate Company' and subsequently applied for planning permission for various lots in succession, both in the company's name and in their own. It seems as if they had formed a sort of 'ring' to avoid outbidding each other and thus gaining a mutually satisfactory low price. Judging from the conveyances to him of 76–80 Aberdeen Road in 1895[13] and by subsequent planning permissions, W. Bibby was brought into this builders' consortium a little later.

The Moorlands Estate was built more or less in accordance with this plan, although there were problems with an unsuspected (or disregarded) cholera burial ground which affected the final layout of Kirkes Road, while there were a number of minor changes on the north-east corner of the development, including the realignment of road junctions, the omission of houses on the East Road frontage and the rearrangement of houses fronting Wyresdale Road to create another street – Tarbet Street – behind. It is clear that the houses fronting Wyresdale Road above and below Christ Church should be seen as part of the same development. The fourteen streets of Moorlands contain a small variety of house types constrained by the bye-laws and by plot-size and rental value, which had by the 1890s become very rigid and standardised. The steep slope on which the estate lies, however, affords some break from monotony and allows more distant views.

Scotforth had seen considerable ribbon development from the 1850s onwards, but here as well there were some larger estates.

Bowerham

Part of the Bowerham Estate adjacent to the new Barracks was put up for sale in the early 1880s. This rather awkward triangular site was initially laid out in lots with street names such as Regent Street and Portland Street, but it was built in a rather different fashion, with names such as Golgotha Road and Adelphi Street, presumably because of the confusion with the Lancaster street names.[14] Because Claremont Terrace was built first, along Bowerham Road, there was a very difficult junction with the first terrace off it, so that Cumberland View seems to be built back to front. This piece of layout was probably illegal under the building legislation since there is no 'front street' as such.

Greaves

At the very end of the century several fields belonging to the Greaves Estate, owned by the Lancaster Charity Trustees, came on to the market.[15] These fields lay to the west of the main road, on both sides of St Paul's church. Those to the north were just starting to be built upon in 1901 with roads such as Bridge Road and Kensington Road, while those to the south are later and in the form of large semi-detached houses.

Meanwhile in *Skerton* there was also a certain amount of ribbon development, along Owen Road, Slyne Road and Aldren's Lane, and some single streets like Edith Street (now Vale Road). However, there were some larger developments.

Lune Street/Derby Road

These streets (Lune Street, Derby Road, Earl Street, Lord Street and Albert Road) were built on the former 'King's Meadow', an estate which fell into the hands of Michael Mattinson Harrison, land surveyor, in 1879. He quickly let out lots to a variety of builders and houses were occupied by the mid-1880s. There are indications that the original intention was to build houses of a greater than average value here, which may account for the three-storey houses and the little touches of pretension such as 'Westbourne Terrace'. One deed relating to Lune Street[16] requires the builder to build houses worth £300 each to a generous specification. It seems likely that Skerton's demands were really for cheaper housing and thus specifications were reduced in later building.

Aldren's Lane area

These streets (Pinfold Lane, Norfolk Street, Broadway, Gardner Road and Olive Road) were built piecemeal in the last decade of the nineteenth century. They represent one of the largest and densest settlements in Skerton and are grafted on to the back of earlier burgage plots relating to the original village of Skerton, represented by Main Street. The new streets, though generally cheaply-built, were solid and of a minimum standard, while the older parts rapidly grew less attractive and became slums, being largely demolished in the early 1960s.

Alexandra Road area

The streets in this area (Alexandra Road, Buller Street, Daisy Bank, Clarendon Road and Ruskin Road) were built on part of the estate of Lune Bank, a large Georgian property which in the eighteenth and early nineteenth century belonged to the Housman family. Building took place in the last few years of the nineteenth century, to the cheapest specification.

House Types

Houses tended to be categorised according to their cost of building and, more particularly, to their annual rental value, from which was calculated their rateable value. The smallest houses tended to have the lowest rental/rateable value and in general size was the important factor, though the size of gardens was also taken into account in working out the value of houses in the Freehold, since occupancy of property above £10 per annum gave a vote in parliamentary borough elections before 1867.

Building regulations, as we have seen, determined certain minimum standards, particularly the size of back yards, the height of rooms and the size of windows in relation to floor area. Beyond that datum line there was a hierarchy of features which gave external indications of the relative value of the house and the status of its occupants.

At the lowest level were those houses built flush to the street, without any garden or projecting windows. Even among these there was some variation in size. These houses can be subdivided according to the position of the stairs, the presence or absence of an internal hall or draught-lobby and the privacy or otherwise of the second bedroom from the stairs. Adjacent houses could have paired doors (i.e. the two houses were mirror images of each other), or doors and windows could alternate, giving the same basic layout for every house. The latter is generally an earlier feature, perhaps ruled out for expense reasons in later developments because the fireplaces and chimneys could not be built back-to-back.

Bay windows were slight indications of a more valuable house, ranging from a timber ground-floor bay, to a stone ground-floor bay, to a full-height stone bay. Most of the earlier bays have hipped roofs, either tiled or leaded.

Front gardens were desirable as a measure of privacy, often, though not exclusively, associated with bay windows. Sometimes the front garden is so small as to be vestigial, as indeed is the bay window. Houses with bay windows often had a porch, rather than just the slightly projecting door-head seen in the flush-built type. By the latter part of the century a standard type had emerged in which the bay window had a pitched roof which continued over the door, either producing a continuous outshut along the front of a terrace, or with each pair of houses treated as a unit.

Quite a high proportion of Lancaster's terraces are of three-storey houses, accounting for the large number of six-roomed dwellings, and here there was an additional hierarchy relating to dormer windows, between those of timber, projecting from the roof, and those of stone with their own gables.

Internally the simplest division is into 'half-hall entry' and 'non-hall entry'. (Muthesius) A hall inside the front door, however small, gave some shelter from the weather when the door was opened, and some measure of privacy for the occupants of the front parlour. Those houses without a hall often had a small draught-lobby just inside the door to avoid wind blowing smoke or sparks from the fireplace, though it is not always clear whether this is an original feature.

It is useful to compare three of the simplest, flush-built, houses in different streets, and of different dates, to see what variations are possible on the plan.

First, 24 Charles St, in the Greaves area, built c. 1880 and relatively unchanged at the time of survey in 1992. Entry is from the street straight into the front parlour, with a small added draught-lobby. A door in the middle of the partition wall leads into the kitchen, where a stair rises from the back corner with a sharp angle. Under the stairs is the pantry. At the top of the stairs are two bedrooms, front and back, and in between them, running up across the width of the house, is another flight of stairs leading to an undivided attic. Down the yard is a w.c. and coal bunker. At the time of visit there was still no bathroom and no water supply except to the kitchen.

Second, 100 Aberdeen Rd, on Moorlands, built c. 1895. Entry is similar to that of Charles St. At the back of the parlour a door leads into the kitchen and also to the stairs down to the cellar from the kitchen. The main stairs run up across the width of the house to the first floor. Here there are three bedrooms, one at the back and two at the front. The smaller front bedroom is built over the passage leading to the back yard, so only alternate houses have three bedrooms.

Lastly, 24 Nun St, Dry Dock, built in the late 1870s. Here entry is into a front hall from which a front parlour and kitchen open. The hall does not extend right through the house (technically it is a 'half-hall entry' house) so a door from the kitchen gives access to an extension containing a wash-house. At the back of the hall stairs lead up to a landing giving access to three bedrooms, the smallest of which is built over the wash-house. A cellar under the house is reached from the back yard, where there is also a brick privy. Like many houses of this type it now has a bathroom in place of the third bedroom.

These three houses show a hierarchy in the use of space and in privacy which is unrelated to their date. No. 24 Nun St is like a small version of the standard late Georgian terraced house. The first house would count as a four-roomed house, the last two as five and six-roomed respectively, but there is considerable variety in the way they achieve this, which in turn affects whether and how they can be modernised, especially in the matter of a bathroom. These are all quite simple houses; many of the contemporary middle-class houses are no more complex, but differ in overall size and spaciousness.

Many of Lancaster's new terraces in the nineteenth century had to be fitted in to quite awkward sites with sharp corners or rising ground, leading to variations in shape and the position of cellar access. The choice of plan and size seems to have been determined firstly by the anticipated status of the development and secondly by the lie of the land. The number of storeys and of rooms related to the likely rent to be obtained. There was no point in building expensive extras which lay outside the financial reach of the anticipated occupiers. Features such as rear access were determined by the presence or absence of another row immediately behind. If there was no access from a back lane then a tunnel would be provided through between houses to the yards behind. This was to avoid the need for ashes or rubbish to be carried out through the house. Passages took a number of forms. A common version in Lancaster (and also in Preston)[17] was a wide, shared but undivided passage through between the houses meeting a dividing wall between the rear yards. Where they met the two gates giving access to the yards were set at an angle to each other, thus allowing a wide opening while still rigorously apportioning the space.

Cellars were often provided and, where the ground fell sharply, the cellar might be provided with a rear access at ground level from the yard. On steeply sloping ground houses were often built in pairs – that is to say that rooflines ran horizontally in a series of steps. This is a quite different tradition from that of West Yorkshire where a sloping terrace often had a continuous roofline parallel to the ground.

Domestic Services

Many present-day occupiers of nineteenth-century terraced houses find it hard to visualise how their houses were used when new and what the occupiers of those days took for granted. This is not helped by the mythology which has grown up around the subject, based on the idea that huge families occupied tiny houses, and a great absence of any written history of the subject. Indeed, we probably know more of the everyday life of very poor rural families from such classics as Flora Thompson's *Lark Rise*[18] than we do of those of more moderate fortune in towns such as Lancaster. Fortunately, we do have an excellent oral history resource created by Dr Elizabeth Roberts in the early 1970s and subsequently used as a basis for her *Working-Class Life in Barrow and Lancaster*.[19] Her respondents included a number of people born in the late 1870s and early 1880s whose testimony is very helpful in establishing how rooms were used and named, and what services were available in the new suburbs.

Right and opposite: Plans of three houses to show the variations possible on the theme of a small flush-fronted terraced house. (Drawn by Paul Thompson)

24 Charles Street

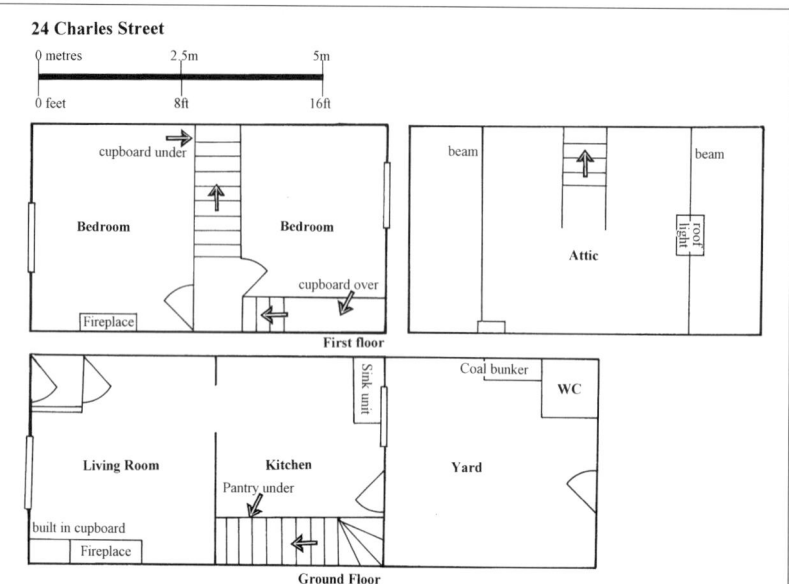

100 Aberdeen Road

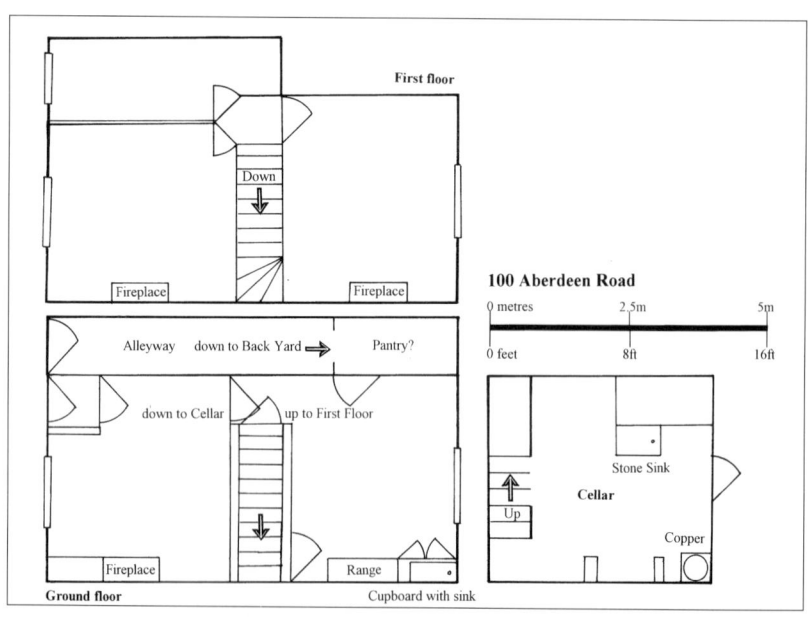

The parlour was frequently, perhaps mainly, used as a best room where visitors were entertained, where courting couples might be left on their own, where coffins stood before the funeral and where mourners met afterwards. As a best room it contained the best, if uncomfortable, furniture and was therefore little used. Mr G.2.L., who was brought up in Skerton, remembers that their parlour was rarely used, being kept for Christmas time or for music. A few better-off working-class families, or those with pretensions to culture, had a piano in the parlour. The separation of functions depended on the house plan and the sort of house that had a

18

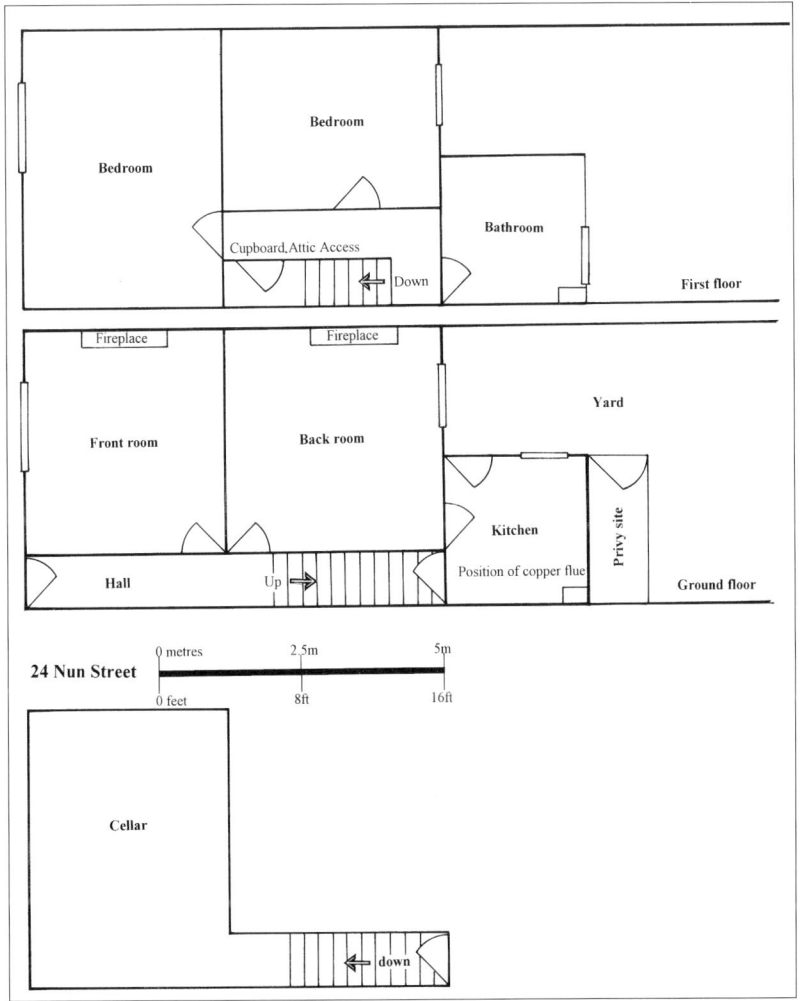

24 Nun Street

parlour accessed directly from the street was more difficult to use in this way. The kitchen was the main living room where the family sat, where meals were cooked, frequently over the fire on a crane in the old way, sometimes in a side oven. Some very poor families used common bakehouses such as the one in Penny Street (Mrs B.1.L.), but these facilities were more commonly used by those who lived in yards nearer the town centre. Usually the only piped water to a house came to a tap over the slopstone in the kitchen. (Mrs H.2.L.)

In the almost universal absence of a bathroom, except in middle-class homes, baths were usually taken in a tin bath in front of the kitchen fire, with water laboriously heated over it or in the wash-boiler. Some people did not bathe at all as we would understand it, relying simply on using a bowl of water for a 'good wash'. (Mrs B.1.L.) There was always some distinction between those families which, however large, managed to take a weekly bath each (Mrs H.2.L.), and those that did not. An alternative for some, principally when the children were older, was to use the public baths in Cable Street. (Mr B.2.L.). Behind the kitchen in all but the smallest houses was usually a wash-house, known in Lancaster as the 'back kitchen'. Here would be a wash-boiler and dolly tubs for clothes washing, and clothes horses or a rack hanging from the ceiling for the clothes to be dried on. Some very poor women carried out washing for others on a casual basis as a means of raising cash in their own homes (Mrs B.1.L.). Clothes could be dried in the back yard in good weather. Earlier, pre bye-law, houses might have a shared drying ground at the rear, like the terrace nos 1–11 St George's Quay.

Also in the back yard would be a privy and ash-pit. In those houses built before the 1850s the yard and privy were often shared; by the end of the century all new houses had their own yards and privies, most of which contained flush toilets. There was a degree of prejudice against inside privies; they were thought to be unhygenic and were quite uncommon before the twentieth century, even though they were quite practicable. Mr G.2.L. describes houses being built on Fairfield as late as 1907 with bathrooms but still with outside privies. Mrs H.2.L. mentions that the shared outside privy used by her own large family and others was very clean, its board seat scrubbed to a smooth finish with soap and soda from the washday. The ash pit was cleared by the ash-pit men who came into the yard carrying large wicker baskets and dug out the ashes and rubbish. Theirs was a filthy job. (Miss H.4.L.) (Mr T.1.L.)

Some houses were lit by gas. Mr T.1.L. recalls having gas light in Garnett Street while his wife, who came from the Woodville area, had been brought up with oil lamps. Some middle-class houses had electricity for lighting before the end of the century, though this was partly a matter of proximity to the electricity station and partly a matter of cost.

Bedrooms were rarely adequate for family size, at least to our standards, and few children had the luxury of a bed to themselves. It was usual in two-bedroomed houses for the parents to have one room and the children another, girls and boys sharing separate-sex beds. Infants often shared the parents' room. Not all families were of conventional structure of course; sometimes three generations lived together, while one or other parent might be dead. There might also be lodgers to be accommodated and so there was no completely standard solution to room use.

Meals were quite a problem for large families. One family shared one big plate of food at the table. The children sat on stools. (Mrs H.2.L.) Parents might enjoy the best chairs, such as a rocking chair and a smoking chair, and in better-off homes there might be a 'nice table with a nice cloth on it' (Miss H.4.L.). Families were not always better-off because they were better paid; some separate skill might attract extra cash, while small families might eat and live more comfortably than larger ones.

Building Materials

Most of the nineteenth-century building work in Lancaster was carried out in local stone. The tradition of stone building for ordinary houses here only goes back as far as the late 17th century when a combination of increasing prosperity and demand for fire-resistance (led by a particularly disastrous fire in Church Street in 1698)[20] meant the rebuilding of what had been a principally timber-and-thatch town. The stonemasons thereafter followed an almost unbroken tradition, interrupted briefly by the twentieth-century's love affairs with brick and concrete, but still continuing in a few hands.

Stone was used because it was available locally and therefore cheaply. Once the tradition was established it was difficult for brick to make any headway and it was used very little – at least as a surface treatment – before 1900. It is noteworthy that even in Accrington, home of one of the most unlovely brick-types ever made, most of the town itself was built in stone. In the eighteenth century only one building of brick was to be seen in Lancaster, and undoubtedly there was a local preference for stone.

The stone was an attractive and easily worked sandstone from the Namurian gritstone series, ranging in colour from almost white to a pale red. It is often marked by bands of distinctive brown iron-staining and weathers to a darker colour, usually grey or golden-brown.

All the quarries lay to the east or south-east of the town, on Lancaster Moor or in Bowerham. The largest was the group owned by Lancaster Corporation on the Moor, known simply as 'The Stone Quarries', or 'The Knotts'. These had been used since at least the early eighteenth century and were usually rented out to a number of stone-masons. It is not clear whether they were worked out by the latter part of the nineteenth century: at all events James Williamson bought out any existing rights in order to landscape the quarries and turn them into Williamson Park. Work on the Park went on from about 1877 until 1882, so effectively the quarries ceased to work in about 1875, before the greatest expansion of suburban building.

One quarry existed above Primrose Hill (now known as 'Scotch Quarry', perhaps because the Scottish-named streets of Moorlands were built from it) and another on the Greaves, a little south of Belle Vue. The latter had been used since the eighteenth century when it was known as 'George Gibson's Quarry'. A further small quarry lay at the top of the Freehold, at the eastern end of Park Rd. This seems to have gone out of use before the 1870s, and so may not have been significant for the greatest mass of building. One at least of the quarries produced a vein of reddish stone in the Victorian period which had not been used in any Georgian buildings except the very latest. Examples of this stone can be seen quite widely, for instance in Marsh Street or in the string courses of Vineyards Terrace, West Greaves, or in what is now the Polish Catholic church in Nelson St. It was also used in Moor Lane Mills. Scotch Quarry was owned in 1896 and 1901 by William Harrison, stonemason, quarry owner and builder. In 1901 Greaves Quarry was operated by John Hatch & Sons. In 1852 there were at least two other quarries at work. It was claimed that there were five others in competition with the Corporation (Moor) quarry, and that stone prices in Lancaster made this one uneconomical to rent even at £52 per annum, whereas it had formerly let for £100.[21]

In many of the terraces of larger houses the stonework was ashlared. Regent St, Morningside and Lindow Square for instance show this treatment, but its appearance is quite different from that of Georgian buildings in the town, the blocks being smaller and the joints being wider. Most are given some surface tooling; there is very little of the flush rubbed masonry used in the previous century. Most other terraces had walling in coursed rubble, sometimes rock-faced.

It is difficult to assess how much brick was used as a cheaper inner skin under stonework. It was certainly used quite widely in rear extensions of stone houses, e.g. in Moorlands or in Percy Road. Brick as the principal building material is confined to a few terraces in Lancaster. One of the most strikingly out-of-place is that in St Peter's Road, which could be anywhere in the Midlands with its red brick and contrasting blue brick dressings. Brick is covered in render at Stanley Place and in the upper storeys of Ayr Street. A house on the corner of Perth Street and Aberdeen Road has a brick side wall. A group in Long Marsh Lane is in red brick. Addle Street, Scotforth, has red brick and render, as does Emerson Street. Brunton Road is in a yellow brick unlike anything else in Lancaster. Decorative terra-cotta tiles are to be seen on the gables of Lansdowne Villas in Regent St. Mercifully there are no examples of the lavatorial shiny white brick so beloved of Victorians, especially at the seaside.

There are indications that brick was edging into Lancaster as a legitimate material by the last years of the nineteenth century and was to become standard during the twentieth century, particularly for council houses and other semi-detached properties, but usually under a coat of pebble-dash. It was available from a number of local sources such as the kilns in the Lune valley at Claughton and Brookhouse or from Scotforth, Glasson Dock or Quernmore.[22] Many of these kilns also produced tiles, drainpipes and chimney-pots. More distant sources are also likely.

Behind the use of the various materials we must consider the falling costs of transport throughout the nineteenth century which allowed building materials from distant sources to be brought quite cheaply to site. This would clearly influence decisions at the cheaper end of the market. At the more expensive end of the market was the taste for diverse materials and eclectic finishes in one building, together with a disregard for the local vernacular. This may account for some of the larger houses in Regent Street or those in Hubert Place. Lancaster was, however, relatively modest in its taste for polychrome design and varied texture. There are few extreme examples, none to be found in terraces (all are detached houses). The more flamboyant tastes are to be found in late nineteenth-century Morecambe, which knew much less restraint.

The carpenter's work in building is rarely obvious from the outside of Lancaster's terraces. It appears mainly in timber bay windows, throughout the period, and in fancy bargeboards and porches, mainly towards the end of the century. Ornate woodwork can be seen in South Regent Street, while elaborate porches occur in Dallas Road and gothic mouldings and trefoils at Hastings and Kensington Roads. Despite the relative unimportance of timber in external details the role of carpenter was an important one, involving roof timbers, joists, floors, doors and window frames and miles of timber scaffolding. Many of the speculative builders were carpenters by trade, and were backed by well-stocked timber yards and sawmills. In 1901 Newsham & Newe were advertising themselves as Joiners & Builders with 'electric saw mills' while in the same year Robert Thompson was offering himself as 'dealer in all kinds of building materials' including 'ready-made English doors, windows etc', as well as acting as a builder and joiner. William Harrison was offering the same sort of service for stone. He was not only a 'builder, mason and contractor' with a steam masonry works, but also supplied sinks, chimney pots and floor tiles.

There has not yet been a detailed study of Lancaster's roofing but it seems fairly clear that by the middle of the eighteenth century the use of local stone roofers (Clougha flags) had ceased within the urban area and Lake District slates, mostly from Coniston, were now easily accessible and cheap, as well as being much lighter than the local product. This enabled builders to construct a lighter timber roof structure and brought a good deal of uniformity into roofing. Welsh slates, such as Velinheli, were also used, and could be obtained from suppliers like William Harrison. The slaters were traditionally also plasterers and dealt in plaster of Paris, hair, nails and laths, like Till & Ripley in 1881. Plumbers and glaziers like Joseph Walmsley provided pumps and water closets, glass, varnishes and colours (presumably lead-based). In small terraced houses their influence was fairly small since piped water was usually delivered only to the kitchen/scullery or to the w. c., if there was one. Glazing was important, however, and changes in technology led to the production of larger and cheaper sheets of glass and also meant that windows needed less glazing bars.

Towards the end of the century the growing standardisation of houses resulting from legislation fuelled a new trade in builders' supplies, largely taken on by new and existing builders. From their wholesale stocks they could build the multitudes of very similar houses and also supply individual wants of the small jobbing builder. There was not yet the slightest hint of do-it-yourself which later changed the role of the builders' merchants so radically. The ease of obtaining supplies attracted many into the trade of builder in boom periods. Finance and connections were becoming more important than skill in the trade.

Building and Planning Control

In the 1830s and 1840s there was a spirit of laissez-faire about building, except where the landowner chose to take an interest, in which case there would be stringent conditions on layout and appearance. A desire to control the quality of working-class housing developed with the recognition that overcrowding, poor drainage, shared privies and bad ventilation encouraged all manner of diseases, including cholera and typhus. Most towns and cities started improving their housing, water-supply, drainage and burial grounds during the late 1840s and 1850s, nudged forward from time to time by national legislation.

In 1844 Richard Owen produced his 'Report in the Sanatory Condition of Lancaster'. In this he mainly attacked the yards and courts occupied by the poorest townsfolk, but he also singled out the terrace of back-to-backs in Factory Hill.

> In Factory Hill, for example, there is a block of eighteen cottages, built back to back. Mr Ricketts, who had here attended some bad cases of children's diseases, drew my attention to the uncleanly state of some of the abodes; and Mr Jackson, the mill-owner, complains that he could not prevent the habit of overcrowding. Two or three families would stow themselves into a space fit only for the wholesome occupation of one family; and though in the receipt of full wages would thus save expense of rent at the expense of health, in order to gain means of indulging in excesses, calculated more directly to undermine the constitution.

The first significant national legislation was the Public Health Act of 1848, which covered many areas of health reform but, as far as buildings were concerned, was mainly permissive of local initiatives rather than compulsory. Even the 1848 legislation was at first dismissed by the Corporation as a luxury, but realisation soon dawned that it would have to take it seriously. The powers were much increased by the Local Government Act of 1858. This included some model bye-laws which could be taken up at a local level, and this was repeated in 1877.[23] Both had effects in Lancaster, since bye-laws were adopted in 1878 for the Lancaster (Poor Law) Union, which significantly included Bulk, Scotforth and Skerton, all at that time outside the borough.[24] New bye-laws were adopted by the borough in 1884 for new streets and in 1885 for streets and new buildings. All of this legislation related to new building and was not retrospective.

Lancaster Corporation had a Plans Committee from November 1880 but no minutes survive before 1882.[25] Its duty was to see that all new building in the borough conformed with the bye-laws and was inspected during construction and before occupation. The Borough Surveyor and his staff oversaw this work. Deposited plans from this period are now in the LRO[26] and seem to cover a longer period than the legislation would lead one to expect.

Much of the legislation was aimed at outlawing back-to-backs (houses built backing on to each other under a single roof) and that other bugbear of early Victorian housing, shared privies and drying grounds. Light and ventilation were safeguarded by wider roads and open space at the rear, while privies and ashpits were to be cleared without having to carry the nightsoil or rubbish through the house. This meant effectively that all houses had to have their own rear yards, accessible either by a back lane or by passages between houses. We can therefore easily distinguish between pre bye-law houses and those built under its controls. The main provisions of the 1878 bye-laws were these:

Streets

- streets to be as level as practicable.
- width to be at least 36 feet if a carriage road.
- streets longer than 100 feet to be built as carriage roads.
- all other streets to be at least 24 feet wide.

- carriage way to be at least 24 feet wide with pavements not less than 1/6 of entire width.

Houses

- control of site, surface, building materials.
- no projections from walls except ornaments.
- damp-proof courses.
- minimum thickness of walls.
- specifications for roofs, chimneys etc.
- open space at rear to be not less than 150 square feet (including w.c. or earth closet and ashpit).
- window area to be at least 1/10 of floor area of room.

These sound fairly modest requirements but they were general and aimed at stopping the worst practices in the country as a whole – not specifically at Lancaster. They had the effect of reducing the density of housing on a given plot and led to a growing standardisation of plans.

Notes to Chapter One

1. A. J. White, 'Urbanism in Lancaster; the building of Dalton Square', *Georgian Group Journal*, 1996 (forthcoming), 118–27.
2. LCC Deeds, 161/5 and 161/8.
3. J. D. Marshall, 'The Story of the Freehold', *Lancaster University; Centre for North-West Regional Studies Bulletin*, n.s. 4 (1990), 19–22.
4. R. Homan, 'The Kendal Union Building Societies', *Trans. Cumberland & Westmorland A. & A. S.*, 2 ser., LXXXII (1982), 183–90.
5. Lancaster Central Library, MS 6566; PL1/63–4.
6. LRO, Rate books 1861.
7. Lancaster Central Library, Scrapbook 1, pt 2, 143.
8. Lancaster Central Library, MSS 5818,5819.
9. Knox-Little *v.* Gregson – 1890 – G. – No. 2092.
10. *Lancaster Times*, 8/9/1893.
11. Lancaster Central Library, S1/25.
12. Lancaster Central Library, PL1/209, dated 1893 in catalogue.
13. LCC Deeds, 87/2.
14. Lancaster Central Library, PL1/200.
15. Lancaster Central Library, S1/42.
16. LCC Deeds, 211/6.
17. S. Muthesius, *The English Terraced House* (1982), 128.
18. F. Thompson, *Lark Rise* (first published 1939).
19. E. Roberts, *Working-Class Barrow and Lancaster 1890–1930* (1976).
20. S. H. Penney, *Lancaster: the Evolution of its Townscape* (1981), 24–8; J. D. Marshall (ed.), *The Autobiography of William Stout of Lancaster 1665–1752* (1967), 120.
21. *Lancaster 50 Years Ago [1852–53]*, Lancaster Guardian (1904), 74.
22. J. W. A. Price, *The Industrial Archeology of the Lune Valley* (1983), 44, 78, 83.
23. S. M. Gaskell, *Building Control: National Legislation and the Introduction of Local Bye-Laws in Victorian England* (1983).
24. Lancaster Central Library, MS 7068.
25. LCC Minute Book 1874–83.
26. LRO, MBLa. acc. 5167.

2

Builders and Backers

Employers as Builders of Housing

In Lancaster the major employers built very little housing for their workers. In this the town seems to contrast very greatly with Preston and some other Lancashire towns, although we should beware of generalisations. The group of 18 back-to-backs in Factory Hill was put up for Albion Mill workers in about 1820 and owned by the proprietors. The Threlfalls built the terrace known as Bath Mill Cottages in 1837 for their mill. By 1901 Lord Ashton owned a few residences like the one at 25 West Road rated at £39 which he rented to his manager, William Atkinson, and which was clearly a favour for a trusted servant. His company also came to own a few blocks of workers' dwellings including the previously-mentioned Bath Mill Cottages, which it acquired along with Bath Mill in 1870, and built a short terrace at Luneside in 1895. Members of the Storey family were equally discerning, the few houses they owned being either inhabited by members of the family or situated immediately alongside their works at 2–8 Edward Street and 5–21 and 22 Springfield Street. It is possible that these properties were bought either because they were not attractive propositions for private landlords, being particularly badly affected by air pollution from the works, or to house the minority of workers who had to live on or near the sites, such as watchmen and boilermen.

Some housing is associated with hospitals; Willow Grove was for key staff at the Moor Hospital while Royal Albert and De Vitre Cottages and

Plan of 7 Bath Mill Lane. (Drawn by Paul Thompson)

Bath Mill Cottages, Bath Mill Lane, built for the Threlfalls of Bath Mill in 1837. These tall and relatively spacious houses pre-date the building bye-laws and are among the few houses in Lancaster built by employers for their workers.

Hibbert Terrace were for staff of the Royal Albert Hospital. All these belong to the last years of the century. Apart from this there is little evidence for employers' ownership. When in the 1930s Lancaster Corporation compulsorily purchased the property in Bulk St and Monmouth St with all the yards and courts behind running up to the canal bank, they acquired it from Storeys, the owners of Moor Lane Mills, whose workers lived there, but they had not owned it for very long.

By and large it seems that workers found their own accommodation in Lancaster. The housing stock seems to have been generally sufficient apart from the two points, in the 1870s and 1890s, when building booms indicate a growth in demand. Workers who rented houses from private landlords were not quite as vulnerable to their employer's control as were those in tied housing, which had its effects on the politics of the town.

The Builders

In the eighteenth century building work in Lancaster had been undertaken by a team of skilled tradesmen led by a stonemason, or occasionally by a carpenter. This process continued into the nineteenth century and the generic term 'builder' only appears in Lancaster for the first time in 1851. From then on some men appear sometimes under a particular trade, e.g. mason, carpenter, slater or plasterer, and sometimes as 'builder'. This probably reflects the way they worked, sometimes carrying out repairs or acting as a specialist contractor, occasionally building a group of new houses as a speculation. This may have had quite a lot to do with cash-flow, for funding the speculative building of a terrace of houses involved a longish wait for repayment. We have no clear idea of the number of builders and their employees because trade directories show a great fluctuation in numbers and many employees would no doubt be taken on for specific jobs, not retained on a payroll. Even their masters seem to have drifted in or out of the trade as it boomed or declined.[1]

Builders bought up land as it came on the market. They did not want too much at a time because their capacity for raising capital and building prior to sales was strictly limited. Their ideal was to buy land, build a few houses, sell them and buy more land. Many landowners were equally willing to sell. Small fields of no special value lying on the edges of the town suddenly became attractive for building.

Landowners were frequently concerned about the quality and value of housing built on their estates, even if they had sold them outright. This was not just a continuation of the eighteenth-century tradition, based upon leasehold where the landowner expected to regain a valuable commodity at some future date, but was a concern about appearances. Control was usually imposed through the use of covenants. When Hutton Rawlinson Ford sold land on the Marsh for the building of Charnley St and Briery St,[2] he imposed conditions. At the former, John Kitchen was to build eight houses of defined minimum size, worth not less than £200 each and there were to be no 'back and front' houses (i.e. back-to-backs). The owners of the Bowerham Estate imposed conditions on John Kitchen and J. D. Pharaoh in The Grove and Dale St in 1888. House designs had to be submitted and approved before building.[3] At Rosebery Avenue in 1897 John Laycock[4] was covenanted to build seven houses like those he had built opposite, each with a frontage not less than

Cromwell Road, photographed by John Walker during construction in the late 1890s. Such views are very rare. To the right the houses are already occupied, while to the left they are still in the builder's hands, with materials lying in the as yet unmade road. (Lancaster City Museums, Walker Collection)

each with a frontage not less than 15 ′ 3″ and a value of not less than £200. Trades and businesses were not to be carried out.

One's general impression is that up to about 1880 most Lancaster builders operated on a small scale, and that after that a series of larger developments called into being more complex financial arrangements and larger firms. On some occasions it is clear that speculative developers hired contractors to build for them; the name associated with the planning permission is not always that of the actual builder but is sometimes the front for a consortium. Planning permission was granted to W. Wilkinson for the whole of Denmark St and Gerrard St, but in practice these streets were the product of much more complex sub-contracting.

In the earlier part of the century it seemed to be common for two or more tradesmen to work in concert. Thomas Rigg and R. Hall, Pye brothers and Thomas & Isaac Mawson worked at Alma Rd, Marsh St, and Shaw St respectively. If they had different trades this meant they could supervise successive stages of building, the masons putting up the shell and being followed by the carpenters and other trades. It also shared the financial burden before income started to return.

Sometimes, as at St George's Quay (nos 1–11), we can see a more complex arrangement, with a co-operative formed by Robert Wilson, joiner and builder, Thomas and Henry Harrison, stonemasons, and Robert Grisdale, plasterer. They took equal shares in the land and materials, and ultimately in the finished houses, Grisdale taking nos 9–11 as his share.[5]

The usual unit of building was the terrace or part terrace, but even these were sub-divided. In the 1850s many terraces seem to have been built in units of two or three houses at a time, which represented the available capital of a single builder. Geography might also dictate a bend in a road, a change of level or a natural division at which a change of builder might occur. This often accounts for minor changes in detailing or occasionally for a larger change, such as one from two storeys to three. It was clearly cheaper to build several terraced houses than the same number of detached houses, quite apart from the greater density and so return on the price of land. Two houses had one party wall, three had two and so on. For convenience the chimneys were usually set back-to-back into the party wall, so the houses were build as mirror-images in pairs, with the front doors paired. On steep slopes this pairing within the terrace extended to the roof, so that the roof line was stepped.

As time went on the demand for houses increased – especially after the 1880s. Clearly the financial arrangements for funding this building boom had to become more sophisticated. In the case of Moorlands the building of fourteen new streets in a relatively short time called for a strategic approach different from that used in coping with single streets. A Moorlands Estate Company was formed, composed of a consortium of local builders, who had joined forces to buy the land for £15,000, no doubt operating as a ring, to keep the price down.[6] Once the overall layout was approved – not without difficulty – the planning permissions for individual streets and parts of streets were sought by individual builders, although even at this level the Estate Co. was occasionally invoked.

In the case of Dallas Rd and Blades St the Corporation bought the Dallas estate of seven acres for £7,000 from G. B. H. Marton of Capernwray, and then sold it in smaller parcels to builders. Such intermediary action was very useful to the smaller builders, who could not otherwise hope to acquire land of this quality. Blades St was all the work of W. Mashiter, but Dallas Rd was divided between him and four other builders – R. Cornthwaite, W. Jackson, R. Baines and F. & R. Wilson.[7] By the very end of the century there were some builders like John Laycock who could cope with larger projects, probably by sub-contracting. The degree of specialisation, the need to deal with large estates, and a more sophisticated financial system led inexorably in this direction, but there were still those who made a small speculation on a few houses. Even in 1907 a speculative builder might sell what he could, rent out what

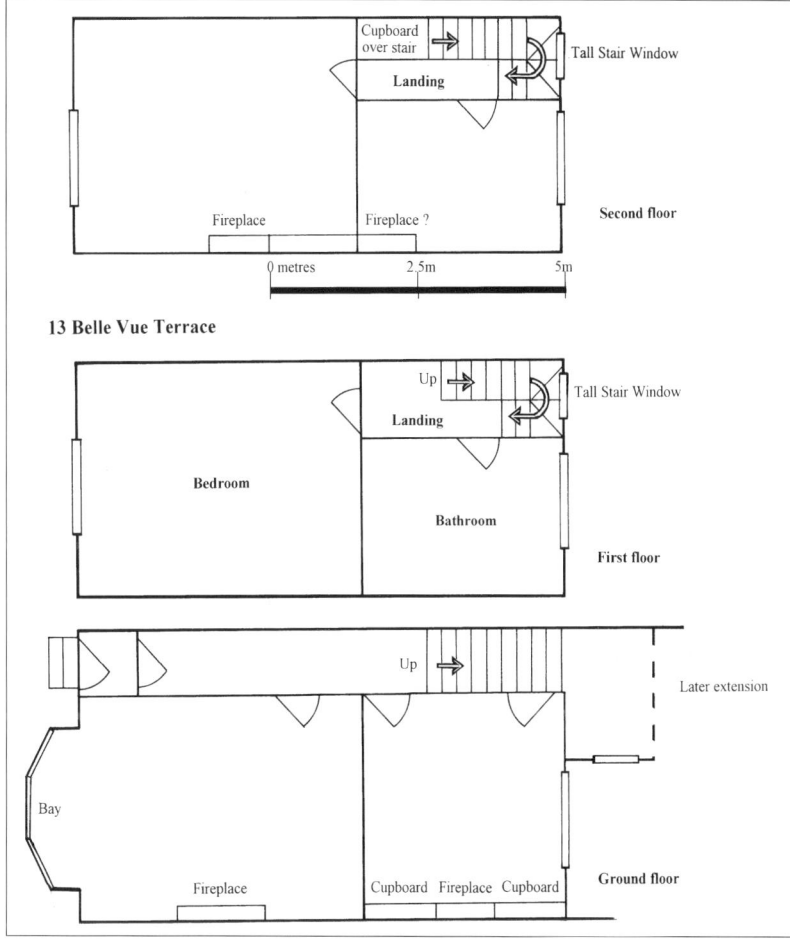

Plan of 13 Belle Vue Terrace, Greaves. The house is more spacious than working-class houses and its style is derived from late Georgian features, including the long stair window at the rear. The name of the terrace comes from that of the earlier house which stands to the east of it, but names such as this did no harm in selling the idea of a suburban idyll to an early Victorian market.

he could not sell, and let vacant houses to his relatives until he could dispose of them.[8]

Sites were often of very awkward shapes because they were mostly acquired a field at a time. Barn Close, behind the present Town Hall, became Marton St/Robert St/Thurnham St while Briery Field became Marsh (Windmill St/Marsh St/Ford St/Briery St/Charnley St). Hubert Place was built on West Paddock. Larger developments were often based upon an estate of several fields or paddocks. These have been examined in Chapter 1.

Street names often immortalise the builder, the landowner or the previous field name, as indicated above. Names of individual terraces are often somewhat whimsical and intended to cast a sylvan touch over the development, like 'Sunny Bank' or 'Halcyon Terrace'. Lancaster cannot match Preston in its deadpan use of terrace names such as 'Hygiene Terrace' or 'Cemetery View' (both off New Hall Lane). In another category were Woodville Gardens, used as allotments by the inhabitants of Edward St and Bath St. Competitions for the best allotment were still being held there in 1880[9] but within two years plans were approved for building four streets on the site (Woodville St/Melbourne Rd/Greenfield St/Williamson Rd). Ford St was named after Hutton Rawlinson Ford, the landowner, while Gregson Rd and Kirkes Rd commemorate respectively the Gregsons of Moorlands House and a Mr Kirkes who had lived at Moorlands with his mother in 1851.[10] Shaw St seems to take its name from John Shaw the builder. Garnett St, Wolseley St, Gladstone Terrace and Hartington St all seem to commemorate figures in the news at the time. Sir Garnett Wolseley was army commander in the Ashanti War of 1873–4 and later Commander-in-Chief. Gladstone was Liberal prime minister and the Marquis of Hartington another important Liberal politician. The Scottish street names of Moorlands reflect the fact that Mr Dowthwaite, one of the principal builders, liked to take his holidays in Scotland![11]

Trade Directories give us the addresses of builders. Sometimes these change, and the change is significant. The new address may be that of new houses that they are engaged upon building. In 1901 W. Bibby's address, and that of A. G. Dowthwaite, are given as Balmoral Rd. Newsham & Newe were also there while A. Cornthwaite was at Dumbarton Rd. All these are known to have been involved with Moorlands estate and the addresses either represent site offices or even temporary occupancy of an end house. W. Mashiter, whose address was Dallas Rd in 1901, was certainly building there – he had gained planning permission for four houses there in 1900–1. As we shall see there was also a notable link between the builder's occupancy of a house as a temporary site-office and that of the corner shop by his wife. In each case the purpose was to save outgoings and to obtain income at a critical financial juncture.

Raising Finance

There were many ways of financing building work, which was considered to be fairly secure, in that it produced a capital asset. Some builders used their own money, some borrowed from family and friends, some attracted sleeping partners and some made private arrangements with wealthy individuals who saw it as a good investment.

One of the ways in which the great mass of Victorian building work was financed was through the Building Societies. These had a quite different function then than now. Instead of helping individuals to buy houses they helped builders to build them, although the mortgage usually took effect when the building was up rather than beforehand.

These Building Societies were able to soak up much of the spare capital of the town, since they represented a good and safe investment. The earliest, the Lancaster Benefit Building Society, appears in the local press in 1837. Soon there were others, such as the Lancastrian BS (1844), the Amicable BS (1844), the New Building Club (1845), Freeholders BS (1849), Alliance & United Benefit BSS (1854), John O' Gaunt BS (1861), Lancaster Royal BS (1863), Lancaster Land & BS Co. Ltd. (1865), Lancaster & District Mutual Benefit BS (1866), Lancaster & County Permanent Benefit BS (1894) and Lancaster Permanent Benefit BS (1895). Some of these clearly emerged from the ashes of others and some may have been short-lived. In 1890 there were the Economic BS, the Lancaster Model BS (which ceased trading in 1900), the Lancaster & Morecambe Investment Co., the Starr-Bowkett BS and the Lancaster & County Permanent BS & IS. The latter was accused of fraud in 1894, an accusation which was subsequently upheld. By 1901 the directories list only two, the First Lancaster Economic BS at 62 Market St, with G. H. Petty as Secretary and the Starr-Bowkett BS at 13 Great John St with R. Roe as Secretary.

In 1845 the Lancaster Guardian commented that the large number of building clubs was leading to a surplus in houses and a fall in rent[12] and later the same year computed that £1/4m was currently invested in Lancaster building societies. A letter in 1863 noted the unfairness of lending money to privileged people.[13] Lists of local Building Societies are given in the local press in 1850 and in 1870.[14] Lists of trustees are also instructive. These are the trustees of the Lancaster United Benefit Building Society in 1849:[15]

John Aldren	druggist
Wilson Barker	mercer
John Moore	ironmonger
John Whimpray	druggist
Thomas Wise	coach builder
Frederick Barker	book keeper
Daniel Simpson	iron founder

These are the trustees of the Lancaster Royal Benefit Building Society in 1857:[16]

Wilson Barker	silk mercer
Christopher Baynes	contractor
James Hatch	joiner & builder
John Moore	ironmonger
Henry Welch	grocer
William Welch	merchant
William Whelon	gent.

The trustees of the John O'Gaunt BS in 1864[17] were:

Richard Hinde	merchant
William Whelon	gent
John L. Whimpray	chemist
Wilson Barker	silkmercer

Most of these are clearly petty capitalists and two have a direct interest in the building trade. James Hatch was also vice-chairman of the John O'Gaunt BS in 1861, and he is known to have been associated with the architects Paley & Austin as woodwork contractor for many churches. There is a considerable overlap in the lists.

Built by the Pharaohs

As will be clear by now, builders, contractors and craftsmen came from a variety of backgrounds and they did not all conduct their businesses in exactly the same way. There was no such person, therefore, as a 'typical' builder and sites were developed by a variety of different means and strategies. Most of these are evident in the careers of the Pharaohs, stonemasons and builders, who operated briefly in Lancaster in the late 1880s.

According to the census of 1891, James Dawson Pharaoh was born at Beckermet, Cumberland, just south of Whitehaven, and Crispin Mounsey Pharaoh at Barrow. They were clearly close relations, possibly brothers, although it is not possible to be more precise about this from the local sources. Both were young married men in their twenties when they came to Lancaster in 1886 or 1887; James's wife, Mary, was from Westmorland, Eliza Pharaoh was from Congleton. Mary Pharaoh had given birth to a daughter, also Mary, at Dalton-in-Furness in about 1885, and was to produce another daughter in 1889 or 1890; Eliza delivered three children between about 1888 and 1891.

In Wells's street directory of 1889 James was described as a builder residing at 2, Adelphi Street, and Crispin as a mason at 114 Prospect Street. These addresses represent the geographical boundaries of their operations as reflected in the building applications which they submitted to the council between 1887 and 1892. In 1887 James Pharaoh and a Mr Morris jointly submitted plans for a row of seven houses comprising 2 Adelphi Street and six adjoining houses in Bay View, Bowerham Road. Morris also applied at about the same time to erect a stable at the rear of the former suggesting that this was also used as the centre of building operations. The following year Pharaoh applied in his own name to build four houses on Adelphi Street (probably 24–30) and in 1889 erected a provender shed adjacent to his stable.[18]

Meanwhile, however, he had purchased a site at the southern end of Prospect Street on 1 November 1887 and had received approval to erect three houses (112–16) on 28 November.[19] These were built during 1888 and early 1889, although only 114 was listed as being occupied in 1889. This site had already passed through

James Pharaoh's house and stable at 2 Adelphi Street.

several hands. It, along with land to the rear fronting Dale Street, had initially been purchased by Edward Thompson, a builder, carpenter and joiner, who had business premises on the corner of Gage Street and Mary Street. From 1886, however, Thompson increasingly directed his attention to developments on the Marsh estate, building houses on Willow Lane, Salisbury Road (1888), Milking Style Lane (1891), and, between 1892 and 1895, most of Coverdale Road (13–45), where he was recorded as living in 1896. The rate book of 1901 shows an E. G. Thompson involved in building the adjacent Gerrard Street.[20] On 13 February 1886 he sold the site in Prospect Street to Andrew DeVarney who was described in the conveyance as a commercial traveller but listed as a foreman painter living at 25 Borrowdale Road in Barrett's trade directory of the same year. It would appear that he was primarily interested in obtaining land to build a house for himself on that part of the site which faced Dale Street since he was resident at 99 Dale Street at the time of the 1891 census. In a conveyance of 1 November 1887, therefore, DeVarney sold that part of the land which fronted Prospect Street to J. D. Pharaoh.

The Pharaohs, however, clearly lacked the finance to develop the site and James again sought a partner. Although an abstract of title for 116 in 1889 cites him as the owner, a document dated 28 January 1888 refers to three houses and a shop in the course of erection by C. M. Pharaoh and Margaret Aldren. It is highly probable, therefore, that the latter supplied the funds which allowed the Pharaohs to undertake the building work. Precisely who she was is not clear, but it would seem reasonable to suppose that she was a member of the Aldren family who farmed in Skerton and after whom Aldren's Lane is named. Miss Margaret Aldren is listed as a private resident living at 3 Windermere Road in 1889 but it may be that this was only a temporary address since Aldren's Lane was then in the process of being developed. Subsequent directories of 1896, 1899 and 1901 record a Miss M. Aldren at 27 Aldren's Lane, as well as other members of the family on the road. On 12 April 1889, 116 was formally conveyed to Crispin, and the following day he obtained a mortgage from the Lancaster Model Building Society, presumably to redeem the loan.

Meanwhile, on 26 March 1888 James had submitted a joint application to build eight houses in The Grove, off Bowerham Terrace, just down the hill from Prospect Street. His partners this time were William Lambert, of Lambert and Moore, ecclesiastical and domestic decorators based in Sir Simon's Arcade, and Edward Taylor, a sculptor and art worker in stone, marble and wood with premises in East Road. Both lived locally, at 1 Dale Street and 5 Springfield Terrace on South Road respectively. The decorative features of these substantial properties undoubtedly reflect the input of his partners. Later the same year, on 30 July, Pharaoh also obtained building approval for three shops on the corners of Westham Street and Eastham Street on the opposite side of Prospect Street from 112–116. These were planned as large, three-storeyed properties comprising a scullery, kitchen and front shop with separate entrance to the ground floor, and five bedrooms above. Only 73 was eventually built precisely to plan, however; 83 was similar, but it lacked the shop front, while the third was never built, the site being incorporated into Yates and Jackson's Park Hotel, built in 1889–90. Finally, on 25 March 1889, just three weeks before he legally conveyed 116 Prospect Street to Crispin, James received approval to build four, three-bedroomed houses between the two properties he was already erecting (75–81).[21]

After he had finished these James Pharaoh left Lancaster. His final application to the council was in July 1892, but this was merely to erect a cart shed behind 2 Adelphi Street which was now occupied by a coachbuilder. In this he described himself as a resident of Over Kellet and the census of the previous year confirms that he moved there before April 1891 since he is returned as 'farmer, quarry owner and innkeeper' of the Eagle's Head Inn. He is not listed in the village in subsequent trade directories, but a Mrs Jane Pharoah (sic) and a mason, John Mark Pharoah, are both recorded in Bulmer's directory of 1912. Crispin, meanwhile, remained at 116 Prospect Street for two more years. In the census of 1891 he described himself as a 'grocer' although the 'shop' at this time was merely the front parlour entered from the hallway, so it is possible that it was run by his wife while he continued to work as a mason in the district, since with a young family she was presumably largely housebound. He was clearly intending to upgrade the premises, however, and on 24 July 1891 he finally received approval for adding two bay windows with a centrally-located shop entrance, together with an extension to provide separate access to the domestic rooms.[22] This work was financed by increasing his mortgage with the Lancaster Model Building Society on 20 October 1891. He then sold the property on 26 May 1893 to the partnership of Messrs J. W. Greenwood and A. Whitehead who installed a resident manager and continued to live in their own houses at 53 St Oswald Street and 1 Belle Vue Terrace respectively. There is no further record of him in Lancaster. In Cook's 1896 directory, however, C. M. Pharaoh is recorded as a 'grocer etc' living at in Clarendon Road, Morecambe, which was then in the course of erection. Three years later a Christopher M. Pharoah, now described as a builder, was living on Chatsworth Road, Morecambe where building was also under way and he was still there, at number 90, in 1901. The combination of retailing and building suggest that this man was Crispin although there is possibility that he returned to West Cumberland around this date since a Crispin Pharoah (sic) is listed as a mason and builder at Santon Bridge, Irton near Gosforth in Bulmer's 1901 directory.

The Pharaohs, therefore, adopted many of the strategies which were associated with small-scale builders at the time. They both lived on site during the course of building and relied on additional forms of income, in this case retailing, possibly generated by their wives: interestingly, 2 Adelphi Street was listed as shop by 1896. They were involved in complex land deals and resorted to both private sources and building societies to finance construction. Furthermore, in common with several other builders including Amos Dowthwaite (Kendal), William Mashiter (Milnthorpe). Richard Paitson Moser (Ulverston), John Laycock (Ingleton), William Singleton (Cockerham) and Thomas and Isaac Mawson (Halton), they originated from Lancaster's traditional hinterland and retained close connections with it.[23] In this respect they were representative of many other men who established themselves in business in the town as it expanded during the late nineteenth century.

Notes to Chapter Two

1. C. G. Powell, *An Economic History of the British Building Industry, 1815–1979* (1980), *passim*.
2. LCC Deeds, 70/7 and 70/50.
3. Lancaster Central Library, MSS 5818, 5819.
4. LCC Deeds, 48.
5. Deeds in possession of Mr R. Stuart.
6. Lancaster Times 8/9/1893.
7. LCC Deeds, 82/1.
8. Centre for North West Regional Studies, University of Lancaster, Oral History collections, interview with Mr G.2.L.
9. *Lancaster Guardian*, 26/6/1880.
10. *Lancaster Guardian*, 6/9/1851.
11. Lancaster Central Library, Obituaries Scrapbook.
12. *Lancaster Guardian* 19/4/1845.
13. *Lancaster Gazette* 31/10/1863.
14. *Lancaster Gazette* 16/2/1850; *Lancaster Guardian*, 26/2/1870.
15. LCC Deeds, 171.
16. Deeds in possession of Mr R. Stuart.
17. LCC Deeds, 21/2/D/24.
18. LRO Lancaster Borough Building Applications (acc 5167), MBLa 341, 15a, 962.
19. Building application LRO, MBLa 849. Other details about this site have obtained from deeds and other legal documents relating to 116 which have kindly been made available to the authors by the owners, Mr and Mrs F. W. Swarbrick.
20. *Lancaster Standard*, 7/4/1893 refers to this business as having been established eight years earlier; an advertisement in the 1889 directory describes the premises as a steam joinery works, with steam sawing, planeing and moulding mills. Building applications for the Marsh, LRO, MBLa 736, 859, 1147, 1255; Lancaster Borough and Poor Rate Book, 1901–02, LRO MBLa/8/49.
21. Building applications LRO, MBLa, 849, 874, 930. Approval for two bay windows to 1, The Grove, was also granted on 25 March 1889: no. 932. Details relating to Lambert and Taylor have been drawn from Wells's *Lancaster & District Directory* (1889).
22. Building applications LRO, MBLa 1239 (Adelphi Street); 1152 (116 Prospect Street).
23. Details about these individuals have been extracted from 1881 and 1891 censuses and from obituary cuttings in Lancaster Central Library.

3

The Terraces' Owners

Landlords

The vast majority of Lancaster's terraced houses were owned by private landlords who rented them out, usually on a weekly basis. This mirrored the national situation. Until the late 1890s increasing demand for accommodation and rising real incomes, combined with low levels of interest and property rates, meant that rented housing was an attractive investment proposition, capable of yielding a steady income while retaining the possibility of appreciating in value over time. Local estate agents, auctioneers and valuers not only acted as intermediaries in the sale of houses, they also published lists of 'attractive' properties for sale or rent and offered, like George Petty of Market Street, to collect rents and to undertake 'the Management of House Properties and Estates' at 'Reasonable Rates'.[1] Such was the level of demand that few houses in Lancaster remained empty for long. Trade directories of the 1890s rarely recorded houses as being vacant; the few that were were generally to be found in middle-class roads where rents were higher and the pool of prospective tenants smaller. Whereas nearly nine per cent of properties in the borough had been uninhabited in the depths of depression in 1861, the figure was only two per cent in 1891, although the extensive building programme underway around the turn of the century pushed the figure up a little by 1901.[2]

It was common for landlords to own only a few houses, often in the immediate vicinity of their own homes or businesses.[3] As late as 1960, sixty per cent possessed just one house and a further twenty per cent just two or three; only one per cent had more than twenty houses.[4] In 1901, the majority still restricted their property ownership to specific parts of town with which they had some association. Cottages in the courts and yards in the older quarters of the town centre had generally belonged to the proprietors of the properties which fronted the main thoroughfares, and this pattern continued to characterise early developments to the east of the town centre like Plumb Street and Monmouth Street, both now demolished. A variant of this emerged in the new terraces where it was common for small-scale landlords to live alongside tenants or in an adjacent street. On the Freehold, for example, residents of houses on the larger corner plots on Borrowdale, Rydal and Dalton Roads in 1901 owned the properties which backed on to them in Grasmere and Windermere Roads. Even more substantial landlords adopted a similar strategy. Among these were men like Josiah Ball, a coal merchant resident at Wender House, Lindow Square who built and owned nine adjacent properties and another on Portland Street; John Dennison, a whitesmith based in Cornmarket Street, who owned nine properties on Albion Street and lived on the junction with Hinde Street where he and his wife also ran a shop; and Thomas Gardner Thompson and his son, Skerton corn millers and flour dealers, who had houses on Aldren's Lane. Others, however, spread their property holdings around town. Luke Gorst, a Penny Street grocer, and his wife Mary, resident on Regent Street, owned nine houses on Earl Street, Skerton and two in Lune Road on the Marsh; Robert George Hoyle, who lived on Blades Street, owned another eighteen properties on Broadway,

LANCASTER
Auction and Agency Offices,
62, MARKET STREET

Telephone No. 71.
Telegraphic Address—"Petty, Lancaster."
(Opposite the King's Arms Hotel).

GEORGE H. PETTY, F.A.I.,
AUCTIONEER AND VALUER,
Insurance and General Property Agent, Accountant, &c.

Branch Offices:—8, West View Terrace, MORECAMBE.

SALES BY AUCTION
—OF—

Estate and House Property, Household Furniture and Appointments, Oil Paintings, Works of Art, Farming Stock, Cattle, and Agricultural Produce, Machinery, Trade Stock, &c., conducted with energy, economy and despatch.

Settlements made on the Day of Sale when required.

VALUATIONS FOR PROBATE, ADMINISTRATION, TRANSFER, AND ALL OTHER PURPOSES, CAREFULLY PREPARED.

Rents Collected, and the Management of House Properties and Estates undertaken at Reasonable Rates.

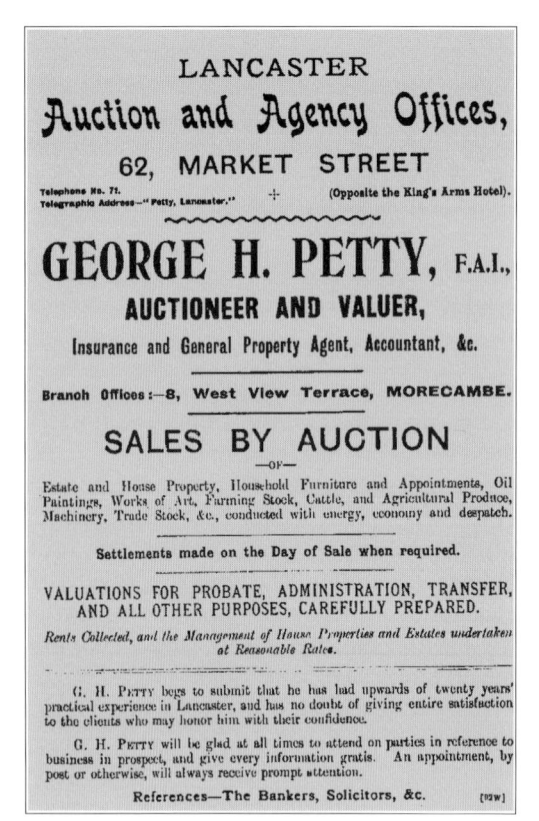

G. H. Petty begs to submit that he has had upwards of twenty years' practical experience in Lancaster, and has no doubt of giving entire satisfaction to the clients who may honor him with their confidence.

G. H. Petty will be glad at all times to attend on parties in reference to business in prospect, and give every information gratis. An appointment, by post or otherwise, will always receive prompt attention.

References—The Bankers, Solicitors, &c.   [02W]

Advertisement for Lancaster Auction and Agency Offices property services, 1901. The name of Petty remained associated with estate agents in the town until the 1980s. (From W. J. Cook's *Lancaster and District Directory*, 1901)

Cromwell Road, Dale Street, Melrose Street, Williamson Road and Windermere Road. John and Christopher Fell, managers of the Jubilee Hall Place of Varieties on Brock Street, dabbled in property speculation in many parts of town, including Skerton, Moorlands and on Brook Street where they lived.

Some of these landlords clearly invested in residential property because it offered an apparently safe outlet for surplus capital during their working lives. It was one of the few ways in which people could provide themselves with a pension for retirement. It is possible to identify several landlords who seem to have adopted this strategy. Thomas Barlow Varley, retired manager of the Phoenix Foundry, who lived at 29 South Road in 1901 owned fifteen houses scattered throughout the town in Skerton, the Marsh, Freehold and on Quernmore Road; no more than three were adjacent to each other. It is also likely that many of the female landlords listed as 'Mrs' in the trade directories of the period were widows who were dependent to a greater or lesser extent on income generated from their housing investments.

Although it is likely that virtually all landlords were local residents, it is difficult to compile an accurate profile of their social and occupational backgrounds. Many were not listed among the 'private residents' in the directories of the time, suggesting that they were of relatively humble origins, while others could have been one of a number of individuals listed with the same surname. The problem of identification is particularly acute in the case of women, very few of whom are traceable. Only a tiny fraction were recorded as being engaged in business, usually as shopkeepers, dressmakers or keepers of apartments. However, it is possible to be more precise about the percentage and value of the new residential and shop property which they held.

Ownership of Rented House and Shop Property built since *c.* 1850 in Lancaster suburbs, 1901.

	% Males	% Females	% Companies, Societies, etc.
No. of properties	82.51	15.53	2.96
Value of properties	83.34	13.60	3.06

Most women's holdings, however, tended to be concentrated on those estates built before the 1890s. Those with houses on the most recent developments on the outskirts, like Rachel and Sarah Jane Calvert, Sarah Ann Kitchen, Sarah Laycock and Sarah Parker, shared the same surname as prominent male landlords or builders, suggesting that this was a way in which their families provided them with an independent, secure private income. The relative absence of other women suggests that their share of the rented housing market may have been eroded by

Vine Yards, West Greaves, built *c.* 1870–71. In 1901 Richard Willis, a railway clerk, lived in number 84 and owned 86 (now 108 and 110). The other properties were in the hands of three landlords, including a James Lord who lived at 76 Regent Street.

Moorgate. A row of ten houses and adjoining shops built in 1885–86 by Richard Paitson Moser, a timber merchant and builder who lived on Borrowdale Road. He died in 1895, but the properties were still in family hands in 1901. The practice of building houses on a raised walkway was sometimes adopted when the land rose sharply from the roadway. The other examples in Lancaster are Gladstone Terrace on Bulk Road and Clarendon Road, Skerton.

the operations of larger male landlords at the very end of the period or that they were seeking alternative investments to provide themselves with an income; the financial press was certainly aggressively promoting insurance and investment portfolios.

The information which can be gleaned about the occupations of male landlords suggests that they were drawn from quite a wide social spectrum. Only a few came from what might be considered to be the town's social elite. Large manufacturers, high-status professionals, and local landowners probably preferred other ways of making money, including selling land around their residences to potential developers. Private residents, that is, those returned in the directory without a specific trade or occupation, were well represented, although it is likely that some of these were elderly, retired individuals. The majority, however, were independent small businessmen with premises in the centre of town, or journeymen-craftsmen and white collar employees some of whom, it would appear from the building applications, had been responsible for erecting the blocks of houses which they owned.

Fragmented patterns of ownership of rented property were most evident on streets built before the massive boom of the 1890s. Twenty people owned the 42 houses on Williamson Road, for example, and none of them had more than four properties, while the 69 houses on Alfred Street, were owned by 46 individuals, only ten of whom were owner-occupiers, and 32 individuals owned the 57 properties on Primrose Street. Some of these were members of families of the builders who had been active in the 1860s and early 1870s. These had similar profiles to other private landlords in that their holdings were either scattered in ones and twos throughout town, or were adjacent to their residences or workplaces. The retention of substantial numbers of properties was not a luxury which such men could indulge in to any great extent. As small-scale operators they preferred, or needed, to sell once they had built, in order to acquire the capital necessary for them to purchase land and materials to remain in business.

The management of domestic rented property, however, was not a responsibility which everyone relished and the returns promised by insurance companies and banks were increasingly attractive as interest rates crept up from the 1890s. Rising levels of domestic rates and the stagnation in the housing market after the turn of the century further diminished the attractions of purchasing house property for rent, as did the growing threat that a Liberal government would increase the burden of taxation and introduce controls over land and property development after 1908. Increasingly, it seems that aspiring property owners were beginning to restrict their ambitions to purchasing their own residences, re-investing any surplus profits in their businesses, depositing savings in one of the increasingly secure financial agencies, enhancing the quality of their offspring's education, or simply indulging in the purchase of the widening range of consumer goods and leisure services. Although small landlords remained numerically predominant, therefore, well into the twentieth century, they accounted for a declining proportion of the rented housing stock. By 1960 the one per cent of landlords who owned more than twenty houses accounted for around 25 per cent of the rented property market.[5]

On the most recent working-class developments of the late 1880s and 1890s a very different pattern of landlordism was beginning to emerge. Individuals with large blocks of houses were particularly evident in Skerton and elsewhere outside the existing borough boundaries. Such men, for that is who they invariably were, were likely to have substantial holdings in several parts of town and to have been involved in the construction of the houses, whether as developers, contractors, craftsmen or merchants supplying materials and house fittings. Some of the properties they are recorded as owning in 1901 had, of course, only recently been completed or were still in the process of construction. This was the case on Blades Street and Meadowside, for example, where the houses which were not owner-occupied were

Spring Bank, South Road. Not surprisingly, most of these houses were owner-occupied in 1901. Among the residents were a bank clerk, corn miller, building surveyor and an architect.

still owned by the builders, William Mashiter, Simeon Waites and Reuben Baines. Other streets still in the process of being built including Alexandra Road [six owners] Denmark Street, [five] Olive Road [three], Regent/Ruskin Road [two], and Clarendon Road, Daisy Street, and Rosebery Avenue [one]. But what is significant is that families connected with the building trade were already substantial landlords in parts of the town which had been developed up to twenty years earlier, suggesting that they were building with the intention of retaining some of the houses to accumulate capital and generate a steady rental income between contracts. William Mashiter, for example, was reported in October 1892 to have built sixty houses on the Primrose Estate; he still owned forty of them in 1901.[6] John Kitchen, whose offices were at 14 Dalton Square, owned half of Briery Street and Charnley Street on the Marsh, significant stretches of Derby Road, isolated properties on Lune Street and Regent Street, and fourteen houses on Dale Street which he had built c. 1888–90. The executors of the estate of Richard Paitson Moser, builder and timber merchant of Borrowdale Road who died in 1895, retained some 61 properties in and around the Freehold district, on Moorgate, Greenfield Street and in parts of Greaves. Suppliers of domestic fittings and appliances also appeared as landlords of houses which had been built for quite some time. Thomas Preston and William Waller, for example, ironmongers and hardware dealers in Fenton & Co., who supplied grates, mantelpieces and stoves, jointly owned all the houses in Morningside which stretched between their own residences at 49 Regent Street and 58 Portland Street respectively. Preston owned properties in Edward Street and Waller some in

Lodge Place on the other side of town, but whether they had been responsible for developing these is not clear.

The largest speculative developer and landlord around the turn of the century, however, was John Laycock, who resided from the early 1890s at 33 South Road. Although he was generally referred to in the trade directories as a coal merchant based in Parliament Street, much of his income must have come from his investment in houses, both as developer and landlord. By 1901 he owned or was in the process of constructing 217 houses with a combined rateable value of £2037. Only one property, a corner house on Ridge Street, was valued at more than £11 10s. and the average was a mere £9 8s. Laycock was exceptional in terms both of his extensive involvement in construction and the sheer number of houses he owned, but he symbolised the concentration of ownership in the rented housing market that was emerging towards the end of the nineteenth century.

Owner-Occupiers

Not all of the late Victorian suburban residential and retail property was rented. Just under 18 per cent was owner-occupied or lived in by relatives of the owners. Not surprisingly, the degree of owner-occupancy was directly related to the value of property. Only around one in fifty of the houses built since the 1850s and rated at £8 or £8.50 were owned by members of the family living in them; the proportion rose to about one in eight of £10 houses, and nearly half of those rated over £20.

Predictably different levels of owner occupancy were also associated with specific parts of town. Home-ownership was primarily concentrated in the most recently built, higher-rated houses in more uniformly middle-class districts, occupied by white collar, service and professional classes. These buyers clearly preferred new property to old, presumably because it was in more fashionable districts and equipped with the latest internal fittings. Because of this, the levels of owner-occupancy did not necessarily increase over time in a district; they could ebb as well as flow. There is nothing to suggest that levels on the established Freehold estate were increasing in the late nineteenth century; just the reverse. On Windermere Road, for example, the number of houses occupied by their owners or

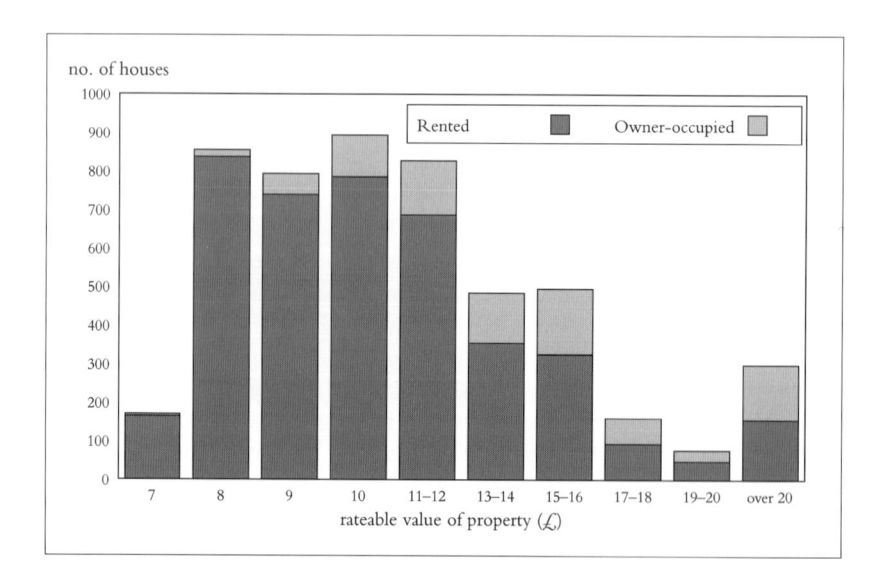

Suburban houses lived in by the owners or members of their families, 1901.

members of their families, fell from 22 to 19 between 1881 and 1911, while the number of rented properties rose from 65 to 72 (an additional four houses were built in the period). The trend was even more noticeable on Ulleswater Road where the numbers were 37 and 28 for owner-occupiers and 62 and 84 for rented properties. Even new streets could experience a decline in owner-occupancy after the initial flurry of purchasers. Although seven properties on Blades Street, for example, became owner-occupied between 1901 and 1911, nine ceased to be.

On the fringes of town, the small number of substantial detached properties rated at £30 or more, usually commissioned by their wealthy prospective residents, were invariably owner-occupied as were a substantial proportion of the terraces which were developed before the early 1880s on South Road, Greaves Road, Portland Street, Regent Street and Lindow Square. These appealed primarily to men who operated businesses on the main thoroughfares of the town, providing an opportunity for grocers, chemists, drapers, furniture dealers and solicitors to vacate the old, cramped, living accommodation above their businesses in the central district for more salubrious quarters. T. D. Smith, a Penny Street grocer, for example, vacated his cottage on Ffrances Passage in 1871 and moved to Vineyard Terrace, Greaves, and then, four years later, to Hermon House, now Victoria House, on Regent Street, where his family had 'comfort, privilege and healthy convenient living'.[7] The steady exodus of similar businessmen from the town centre is clearly evident in the census and trade directories of the period.

Many of the properties rated over £15 built in the late 1880s and 1890s on Dallas Road, Blades Street, Cromwell Road, Aldcliffe Road, Meadowside, Dale Street, The Grove, Fern Bank, Lily Grove, Thornfield, Slyne Road, and Edith Street were owner-occupied by 1901 as were parts of Bowerham Road, Willow Lane and the Moorlands Estate. Although these attracted independent businessmen, they were increasingly bought by white-collar commercial and professional groups including journalists and reporters, artists, commission agents, commercial travellers, drapers' and grocers' assistants, overlookers and office clerks of all descriptions. These people's aspiration to home ownership was a precursor of developments later in the twentieth century which were not unique to Lancaster. During the 1890s their apparent pretensions to gentility attracted widespread contemporary comment, and even ridicule; they were immortalised in George and Weedon Grossmith's cruel satire of the fictitious London bank clerk, Mr Pooter, which appeared as a series in *Punch* and was subsequently published as *The Diary of a Nobody* (1893).

About eighteen percent of the houses lived in by the owners or members of their families in 1901 belonged to women, but their pattern of property holding was distinctly different from that of their male counterparts. Men were much more likely to be named as owners of the most recently-built properties; those owned by women tended to be in parts of the town built before the 1890s. Houses in which female owners' relatives were listed as occupiers also tended to be concentrated in the lower reaches of the market, suggesting that many of them belonged to widows of modest means who had possibly inherited property from their husbands but lived with adult offspring who were listed as the occupiers in the trade directories. As the town expanded, therefore, property ownership spread beyond the independent business class to incorporate white-collared, salaried employees. There is nothing to suggest, however, that it became less male-dominated; indeed it is possible that women were becoming even more marginalised around the turn of the century.

Notes to Chapter Three

1. W. J. Cook, *Lancaster, Morecambe and District Directory* (1901), 137.
2. The figures have been calculated from housing tables in decennial census returns.
3. All information about ownership has been extracted from the Lancaster Borough and Poor Rate Books for 1901–2. These were the first such records to include those parts of Skerton, Bowerham and Scotforth incorporated into the borough in 1900: LRO, MBLa/8/48, MBLa/8/49.
4. J. B. Cullingworth, *Housing in Transition*, 104.
5. ibid.
6. *Lancaster Guardian*, 1/10/1892.
7. Autobiography of T. D. Smith in the possession of the family.

4

Servicing the Suburbs

Until the 1870s, shops, pubs, schools and churches catering for the material, educational and spiritual needs of the population were overwhelmingly concentrated in the central districts of the town. Suburban expansion naturally encouraged the development of more dispersed retail premises to tap the increasing spending power of the residents, but it placed considerable pressure on those institutions which had previously monopolised the religious and educational provision.

Shops and Street Traders

Hawkers, itinerant traders, delivery men and errand boys, were regular visitors to these streets well into the twentieth century. Many of the people interviewed by Elizabeth Roberts refer to coalmen, to bakers with their bread vans, and to salt carts carrying blocks of salt from which chunks were broken off. Perishable produce like milk, eggs and butter was often brought round by farmers, some of whom delivered to local shops. Hawkers also brought fruit to the back door twice a week, and vegetables were sold by local allotment holders. Market gardeners were to be found all around the town, especially along Aldcliffe Road, Milking Style Lane, and in Scotforth and Skerton. One lady, who lived on Wingate-Saul Road just before the First World War, recall regular visits from a horse-drawn fish cart driven by a 'funny old man' who sold cockles and mussels.[1] Further supplies could also be obtained from the covered market in the town centre which was considerably expanded in 1879–80 to cope with the growing demand, or from the twice-weekly street market. On Saturday night in particular there were bargains to be had as traders sought to clear their stalls for the weekend. The presence of so many local suppliers of fresh produce undoubtedly accounts for the relative absence of suburban dairymen and greengrocers in the new suburbs.

There were few retail outlets in middle-class districts since their residents were wealthy enough to tempt town-centre tradesmen to send representatives to collect orders and to offer frequent delivery services. Shops were an integral part of the working-class communities, however, and many people recall that, as children, they were always being sent on errands by their mothers or neighbours. These shops are often portrayed in near identical terms: small, general, corner grocers 'where you could get nearly everything', often run by women whose families lived on the premises, places where the business of buying and selling was inextricably entwined with the exchange of domestic news and gossip. The reality is more complex. Not all of these shops were small by contemporary standards, nor were they invariably situated on corners. There were specialist traders as well as grocers, and they were sometimes branches established by town-centre shopkeepers who were anxious to ensure that they participated in the growing residential market. Nor were they randomly dispersed throughout the town; suburban shopping centres were even emerging by the 1890s.

There is no doubt that small, general retailers were the first to colonise new estates. As we have seen, in some cases wives of small-scale

Ford Street, Marsh

Norfolk Street/Owen Road, Skerton

Prospect Street, Primrose

Vincent Street/Langley Road, Primrose

Corner shops. All were built between *c.* 1875 and 1892. Those on the Primrose were initially operated by builders.

builders living on site ran general shops and other similar, short-lived ventures were evident in the early stages of every development, run by workers' wives, widows or the elderly. These tended to disappear as more substantial competitors moved in once an estate had been completed. This process is clearly evident on Primrose during the 1880s and 1890s. In the 1891 census, for example, there was a shop at 18 Primrose Street run by Jane, wife of Abraham Bleasdale who was returned as a letter press printer. He was credited as a shopkeeper in Cook's directory of 1896 but the business had disappeared by the time of the 1901 directory in which he was simply described as a foreman. Rather more substantial was Alice Pym's shop just up the road at the corner of Prospect Street. In 1891 she was a 54-year-old widow, sharing the premises with another young widow of 26, described as a domestic servant, and her four-year-old son. Widow Pym's shop had been taken over by a town-centre grocer by 1896. By then, however, other shops run by women had appeared further up the hill at 14 Langley Road and 34 Hope Street. These, in turn, had vanished without trace by the end of the century. What is significant about all of these shops, with the exception of Mrs Pym's, is that none of them was rated as a retail business in the rate books; they were all houses situated in the middle of terraces, and they show no sign of ever having been externally adapted for the purposes of trade. As such they probably involved nothing more than a temporary, makeshift adaptation of the front parlour. Significantly, only eleven of the suburban shopkeepers listed in Wells's directory of 1889 were still described in the same terms twelve years later and only six of their premises were still run by members of the same family. Four had been converted to specialist outlets, thirteen had reverted to private residences, occupied mainly by labourers or widows, and the rest were now described as 'grocers'.

Another profitable use to which the front parlour could be put was dressmaking. It is impossible to gauge the precise extent of this trade since it was not consistently recorded in the directories, but it undoubtedly continued to provide an opportunity for women to earn an income at home up to and beyond the First World War. Several of Elizabeth Roberts's interviewees refer to having clothes made up by local women. But it was a trade which was already coming under threat from ready-made clothing in the 1900s and it was destined to be yet another example of that increasing separation of work and home which had undermined married women's opportunities to undertake other remunerative employment.

The location of a shop was crucial if it was to survive for any length of time. Only a few longstanding businesses, such as those at 29 Earl Street, 15 and 71 Windermere Road, 77 Grasmere Road and 40 Norfolk Street were situated in the middle of residential streets. Those on the Freehold possibly survived because corner sites had already been developed as substantial houses. Some, like the store at 36 Westham Street, were adjacent to back alleys which gave access to other streets, but purpose-built shops were usually strategically situated on corners where they could capture the trade of several roads. Such shops, however, were not evenly distributed throughout the new suburbs. Recognisable shopping centres developed at key locations in the town from the late 1880s. In Skerton, the retail premises adjacent to the Skerton Hotel were redeveloped in 1887, and those on the corner of West Road and Willow Lane on the Marsh between 1887 and 1890. As the Primrose estate matured, clusters of shops had emerged by 1895 at the junctions of Prospect Street with Eastham Street, Westham Street and Clarence Street. On the Moorlands estate they were located along Dumbarton Road. Shops at the end of Ulleswater Road and along the adjacent Moorgate nearly all originate from the mid-1890s. Lock-up premises were erected at the end of Ulleswater Road in 1894 and the grocer T. D. Smith put up the corner shop and the adjacent property on Moorgate the following year. At the same time, those next to the Gregson Institute were rebuilt as a direct result of a council initiative to widen the road and establish a uniform building line. It purchased existing premises from their owners for £900 and sold them back to John Singleton, a fancy goods dealer in Stonewell who also ran a grocer's shop on Moorgate, for just £100 on condition that he built shops in line with council requirements. The council's involvement is suitably commemorated by a plaque above the newsagents at the corner of Bath Street. By 1901 the terrace of shops on Greaves Road opposite Belle Vue Terrace was also emerging. During the 1900s houses at the top of Bowerham Road were gradually converted into retail outlets.

Most of these shops were planned with living accommodation above and to the rear which was generally, although not universally, occupied by the shopkeeper's family. On corner sites the residential quarters were entered from the side street through a separate door from that used by customers, and internal access to the shop was provided from the living room or hallway. The street frontages were specifically designed for displaying goods and the shop entrance was often set across the corner of the site. The house and shop erected on the corner of Rydal and Ulleswater Roads in 1873 by William Wildman, for example, had protruding shop windows to both streets covered with a separate slate roof. Access to the house was from Rydal Road and led on to a separate hallway with doors off to shop and kitchen. The shop itself measured some 20 feet by 16 feet. Upstairs there were five bedrooms. Even this was not spacious enough for its first occupant who added a third floor in 1877. The house and bakehouse at 40–42 Clarence Street, erected by Thomas Wearing in 1891, was equally spacious. Downstairs there was a separate hall with doors leading into the parlour and a kitchen with a back scullery and separate access to the bakehouse which had an integral oven; upstairs there was a front parlour and four bedrooms, one of them directly above the oven.[2] These corner shops, then, were often significantly larger than the terraced houses on to which they abutted, reflecting both the importance of their retail trade and the social standing of the shopkeepers who occupied them. They were largely owned and frequently run by men.

Traders who sold higher-order goods like clothing, furnishings and fancy goods remained largely concentrated along the town's central thoroughfares, but a few did appear in the suburbs. The chemist shops on Ulleswater Road and Prospect Street were initially owned and run by William Arkle and William J. Lund, both of whom also traded in Penny Street and who lived in impressive residences on Quernmore Road and South Road. There were also drapers by 1901 on Mill Street, Moorgate, Owen Road, Ulleswater Road, and West Road. Each working-class district managed to provide enough custom to support at least one bootmaker, repairer or clogger. Like the dressmakers, these did not require purpose-built premises and usually worked from their houses. Only 116 Ulleswater Road came close to resembling a shop and significantly this was owned by a local leather merchant in 1901, Frank Cockeril, suggesting that it was effectively an outlet for his wares.

Every estate, however, had several grocers and provision dealers. The biggest operator with branches throughout the town was the Lancaster

Co-operative Stores, corner of Stirling Road/Argyle Street, Moorlands. Above the entrance is a beehive, symbol of co-operative industry, the date (1898), and a plaque which reads 'Lancaster and Skerton Equitable Industrial Co-operative Society Ltd'. This is still a busy shop but is now in private hands.

and Skerton Co-operative Society. Prior to the 1880s its operations in Lancaster were confined to its main premises on the corner of New Street and Church street and a shop at the corner of Lune Street and Owen Road, Skerton. From 1885, as its membership expanded, it rapidly built up an extensive network of outlets. It achieved this initially by acquiring properties which were already trading as private shops in established parts of town: Lodge Street (June 1885), Edward Street (1886), West Road, Marsh (January 1887) and Ulleswater Road (1889), substantially redeveloping the last two within a few years of acquiring them. Thereafter it moved into the suburbs as they developed, erecting purpose-built premises on Prospect Street (1888), Broadway (1892), Green Street (early 1890s), and Stirling Road (1898). Its expansion continued into the 1900s with new shops in Bowerham (Coulston Road), Greaves (Bridge Lane) and Fairfield (Sibsey Street). Each of these branches was run by a resident, male manager, usually living above or adjacent to the shop, and staffed by male assistants.[3]

The significance of the co-op's colonisation of the suburbs was soon recognised by its major competitors some of whom retaliated by establishing their own branch shops, again staffed by resident male managers. T. D. Smith of Penny Street provided the most vigorous response with branches on West Road (August 1888), the corner of Dale Street and Bowerham Terrace (November 1888) and Owen Road, Skerton (February 1889). Premises at the corner of Moorgate and Ulleswater Road (February 1895) were 'newly built for our trade', and in May 1898 a double-windowed shop on the corner of Dumbarton Road and Stirling Road on Moorlands was acquired. Smith in turn attracted imitators, some of them, to his obvious annoyance, men who had 'previously been trained and in the employ of our own business and firm'.[4] William Oldfield, his first apprentice, a grocer based in Stonewell, is recorded in Wells's 1889 directory as operating a branch at 2 Primrose Street, at the other end of Dale Street, and by 1901 he owned a shop which traded under its tenant's name at 2 Green Street but for which he possibly acted as a wholesaler. William Hutchence, another Penny Street grocer who also had a branch in Morecambe, purchased Alice Pym's shop on the corner of Prospect Street sometime in the early 1890s. The James Wilson recorded in 1901 as owning the post office and grocers on the corner of Salisbury Road and West Road on the Marsh run by Richard Wilson, as well as the shop and post office at Scotforth, was quite possibly the grocer and provision dealer listed in King Street.

Other businessmen relied exclusively on the suburban retail trade. Between 1896 and 1901 Richard Gorrill Towers, a distant relative of the T. D. Smith, rapidly acquired a chain of nine shops, usually in existing retail premises. He was exceptional in that he employed manageresses to run them, but the shops were generally in small, inconveniently-situated converted houses and this probably accounts for his disappearance sometime in the early 1900s. James Greenwood and Alexander Whitehead, who purchased 116 Prospect Street from Crispin Pharaoh in 1893, were more successful, branching out from there to buy grocers' shops at 1 Main Street, Skerton, 88 St Leonardgate and 69 Penny Street. In addition to these there were many more property-owning grocers who operated successfully for many years from prominent corner sites in the suburbs.

Some of the butchers based in the market hall also opened branches. James Dixon, and later his widow, ran a shop at the end of Lune Street, Skerton for many years; William G. Barrow traded from Dumbarton House at the corner of Aberdeen Road; the Walling family had a shop in Garnett Street, and John Earnshaw established himself in purpose-built premises at 98 Prospect Street. Although national multiples tended to concentrate on town-centre sites, one of them, Eastmans, briefly rented the adjacent property (96) to Earnshaw in the mid-1890s. In the 1900s these men were joined by others who abandoned the town centre entirely: William Redwood moved from Penny Street to the top of Balmoral Road and George Kuhnle, a pork butcher, transferred his business to Bowerham. Like grocers, a few butchers relied entirely on suburban trade. William Woodhouse, for example, was prosperous enough by the 1890s to move his residence to Meadowside when the lock-up shop opposite his previous premises at 99 Ulleswater Road was built, and to purchase several houses in various parts of town which he let to tenants. James Bibby of Norfolk Street and William Gardner of Moorgate were other men sufficiently wealthy to purchase their own properties during this period.

What might now be called 'fast food' outlets were also increasingly evident. Bakers and confectioners were initially major providers of this. Thompson Gladstone, baker, grocer and beer retailer, erected a shop, bakehouse, oven and stables on Pinfold Lane, Skerton in 1889 and rapidly developed an extensive wholesale trade. As estates matured, the council approved building plans for small bakehouses and ovens attached to properties in Grasmere Road (1873), Charnley Street (1877), Prospect Street (1881), Wolseley Street (1877/1881), Bond Street (1882), Railway Street (1887), Williamson Road (1890) and Clarence Street (1891,see above), the latter two both owned by Ellen Salkeld in 1901.[5]

From the mid-1890s, however, bakers were supplemented by very different catering outlets which were rapidly to outnumber them. These were the fried fish-and-chip shops. Although slower to develop in Lancaster than in the cotton textile towns further south where they had first appeared in significant numbers in the mid-1880s, once they were established they increased rapidly from just seven in 1896, when they were first listed as a separate category in the trade directories, to 25 just five years later and 37 by 1912.[6]

Fish-and-chip shops had their origins in a number of technological innovations in the 1880s, most notably the advent of refrigeration, which transformed the fishing industry and its distribution network. The trade's low capital requirements and heavy labour input appealed to those who previously might have considered opening a beer shop or general shop. With much trade taking place in the evening it was possible for men to engage in paid employment during the day and to assist in the shop after work. The shops thrived on workers' preference for hot, fatty, pre-cooked food, their increasing ability to purchase it, and their need to obtain it close to their homes. As a result of these unique circumstances, fish-and-chip shops were the only retail outlets which were more numerous in the residential areas than in the town centre.

Between 1896 and 1912, ten premises in the town which had previously traded as grocers or general shops were converted into fish-and-chip shops. These included several on the important corner sites including those fronting Green Street and Old Caton Road in Bulk, Dalton Road and Grasmere Road on the Freehold, Garnett Street and Mill Street in Dry Dock, Dumbarton Road and Balmoral Road on the Moorlands, Clarence Street and Hope Street on Primrose, and Albert Street and Earl Street in Skerton. Yet others, on Salisbury Road, Havelock Street, Alexandra Road, Windermere Road, Prospect Street and Langley Road were adapted from private houses although these, like the unskilled general shopkeepers operating from domestic front rooms, tended to disappear within a relatively short period. From the late 1890s, the smell of fried food permeated the streets on the new estates almost as soon as they were complete, with shops being established on Elgin Street and Gregson Road by 1901, and Denmark Street, Sibsey Street, Ash Grove (Greaves), Devonshire Street, Newsham Road and Coulston Road between 1901 and 1912. Lancaster's longest established surviving fish-and-chip shop would appear to be 37 Moorgate, which opened sometime before 1899, but at least seven others can be traced back to at least 1912. They have proved to be an enduring feature of the urban residential landscape.

Lodgings, Pubs and Off-licences

Another use for residential property was the provision of rooms or apartments. Householders with spare accommodation often supplemented their incomes by taking in lodgers who were usually single, male adults attracted to the town by employment opportunities but unable or unwilling to rent their own houses. Some of the larger premises were deliberately taken by spinsters and widows with a view to subletting or providing room and board. Virtually all the widows under the age of 65 listed as heads of household on Ulleswater Road in 1881, for example, took in lodgers, although only a minority specifically returned themselves in the census as lodging house keepers. Women continued to dominate the provision of such accommodation long after this, but the business also increasingly attracted male entrants and this probably accounts for the inclusion of 'Apartments' as a specific category in the trade directory of 1912 when 22 keepers of rooms were listed, nine of them men.

Prior to 1869 another way of generating income from residential premises was by opening a beershop. The Beer Act of 1830 had made it possible to sell beer, but not wine or spirits, for consumption on site by making a simple application to JPs and paying a small annual fee for a licence. Several beershops were established in Lancaster between these dates, but most were in the centre and, since the town was already well supplied with fully licensed premises to service its long established market and social functions, they were never as significant as they were in some of the cotton towns. The lack of substantial residential development before 1869 meant that the only beershops established outside the town centre were the Britannia and Freeholders' Arms.

Unlike beer retailing, the fried food trade and the provision of lodgings, where there were few barriers to entry, the numbers of pubs and off-licences were strictly controlled by local JPs sitting at the annual 'brewster sessions'. Off-licences were introduced by William Gladstone in his budget of 1862. Although middle-class districts of Lancaster remained obstinately dry, JPs sanctioned the establishment of several in the new working-class estates. With the solitary exception of the shop at 88, Windermere Road, owned and run at the turn of the century by Herbert Robert McMullen who described himself as a 'brewer, wine, spirit, ale and porter merchant', these were invariably run in conjunction with other businesses, usually by grocers. The large brewers were acquiring outlets by the end of the century. The shops at 2 Ulleswater Road and 16 Charles Street were in the hands of William Bell, a brewer and wine-merchant on Penny Street. William Mitchell acquired

Pubs. The domestic style of the earlier Rose Tavern, Ulleswater Road (left) contrasts with purpose-built Victoria Hotel, West Road (right). Both pubs were owned by William Mitchell in 1901.

49

Off-licences. The imposing frontage of the grocer's and beer off-licence at 16 Charles Street, Greaves (left), around the turn of the century (now demolished) has similarities with the property which survives as a private house on Windermere Road (right). (Lancaster Central Library and author)

premises in Brunton Street in 1901. The social standing and reputation of the person applying for a licence was taken into account by the JPs when they were deliberating whether to grant a licence. It was difficult for the small man without capital or connections to enter the trade as William Stephenson, a 44-year-old railway engine driver living at 44 Bradshaw Street, discovered when he applied at the brewster sessions in August 1892. Less than two months later, however, the bench allowed William Mashiter to transfer a licence from a shop in Ripley Street, in a relatively poor area adjacent to the Pointer, to his premises on the corner of Vincent Street just up the hill from Bradshaw Street. The fact that he had built upwards of 60 houses in the area undoubtedly assisted his application.[7]

The relationship between big business and politics also determined the nature, pattern and timing of public house development in the suburbs. Pubs established before the 1890s, like the Rose Tavern, functioned in premises which were virtually identical to the houses around them. This establishment, along with the Britannia and the Freeholders' Arms, were initially independently owned, but by 1901 all three were in the hands of the major brewers: William Mitchell (Rose Tavern), and Yates & Jackson (Freeholders and Britannia). Such acquisitions reflected the brewers' policy of buying up small beershops and pubs and then obtaining permission from the JPs and council to extend and improve them. On the more recent estates, however, they had an opportunity to erect purpose-built establishments. Much to the irritation of the temperance movement, which wished to keep the suburbs completely dry, the brewers literally had the JPs over a barrel, since they astutely coupled their licence applications for new hotels on the outskirts of town with a promise to close smaller, presumably less profitable and certainly less savoury premises in the centre of town.

Yates & Jackson first applied for a licence for the Park Hotel in 1889 but were refused on a technicality. When their application was resubmitted the following year the building was nearly complete and described as a 'really good and handsome and substantial hotel' by their counsel. To spike the temperance lobby's guns, they stressed the provision of a separate jug and bottle 'entirely for the outdoor trade', which meant that 'children would not have to go in the public part of the house' with their jugs to obtain beer for their parents. They also promised to close the Volunteer Inn on China Lane, which was described as an 'objectionable neighbourhood' of town, and which they knew the borough council was hoping to demolish. Their application was vociferously opposed by the military authorities at Bowerham barracks, who felt it would be 'a great temptation to the younger soldiers', local builders (and beer retailers) like William Mashiter who argued that the value of neighbouring property he had erected would depreciate, and all the local churches who claimed, in the word of the Wesleyan minister, that it would 'hinder their efforts to secure the moral and spiritual well being of the people of the neighbourhood'. Nevertheless, the JPs clearly had no option but to grant the licence.[8]

William Mitchell's application for the Victoria Hotel at the same sessions in 1890 proved equally unproblematic since he, too, promised to close the Hole in the Wall on China Lane. His licence application for the Moorlands Hotel in 1895, however, prompted the temperance society to accuse the council of conspiring with the brewers against the public interest. By then the council had purchased and demolished nearly all of China Lane, but the substantial Feathers Hotel on the corner of Market Street still stood. Mitchell, the licensee, was demanding a considerable sum from the council if the building was demolished, to compensate him for loss of future revenue. Some councillors, therefore, informally approached the JPs to see if they would transfer the Feathers' licence to the Moorlands. Despite a vigorous campaign by the temperance society, local churches, and their allies on the council, the granting of the licence for what was described as a 'first class hotel' was never really in doubt, especially when Amos Dowthwaite appeared for the estate's developers to support it.[9] Over the next decade and a half Mitchell progressively outpaced his local rival, opening new hotels in Bowerham and Greaves.

Churches and Schools

The alliance of business and politics, therefore, proved too powerful for the self-appointed champions of public morality. The concerned parties, however, did much more than simply oppose licence applications. Churches viewed the new suburbs as an opportunity and a challenge: an opportunity because for the first time people were removed from the apparent demoralising influences of town-centre life; a challenge because they were also physically distanced from existing places of worship. Although the scale of the churches' efforts may appear insignificant in comparison to the much-publicised evangelical missionary work in city slums elsewhere in the country, they were nevertheless considerable when placed in their local context.[10]

Since there was no financial return on the investment, there was no prospect of attracting commercial funding, so they had to rely on the generosity of their members to provide the wherewithal to establish a physical presence. Poorer, smaller sects naturally found this difficult and they largely remained confined to the vicinity of the town centre. The Primitive Methodists channelled their efforts into expanding the Sunday School in Edward Street and into redeveloping their premises on Moor Lane during the 1880s and 1890s, and then opened a chapel in Skerton in 1903. The United Methodists, short of cash, ran a small mission attached to one of the houses in Wolseley Street (no. 6) which was extended in 1892. The Congregationalists had the backing of the Dawsons of Aldcliffe Hall, and they were particularly outgoing in the 1870s, establishing Sunday schools and missions on St Leonardgate and Aldcliffe Lane, as well as building the Centenary Church at Stonewell from which they launched the Pleasant Sunday Afternoon in the 1890s in the adjacent Cromwell Hall, but they did not really venture further into the suburbs

St George's Mission Church, Willow Lane, Marsh, designed by Paley and Austin and erected 1897–98.

until 1901 when they established a presence in Bowerham. The Moorlands 'Tabernacle' on the corner of Balmoral Road and Dumbarton Road was built in 1897 to house the Church of Christ, small sect which had first appeared in Lancaster eight years earlier, but it was a plain, purely functional building of wooden construction.[11]

The battle for souls was waged largely between Anglicans, Wesleyans and Catholics, all of whom possessed the resources to carry the crusade deeper into the suburbs. These gradually extended their premises and replaced small-scale provision in, or adjacent to, houses with purpose-built churches and halls.

The Anglicans were first on the scene and were assisted by some wealthy local patrons. Samuel Gregson provided land and resources for the building of Christ Church in the 1850s while Edmund Sharpe, the architect and entrepreneur, was instrumental in the erection of St Paul's Scotforth in 1876. Thereafter, new church building ceased but concerted efforts were made to enlarge existing places of worship and establish 'missions'. During the late 1880s the vicar of Christ Church opened a mission room at 2 Hope Street on the Primrose Estate and acquired the Gregson Memorial Hall on Moorgate. The latter was designed by the renowned local firm of architects, Paley and Austin, and then partly let out to the Lancaster Coffee Tavern Company as a temperance refreshment house in the 1890s. In 1891 he again recruited the services of Paley and Austin to design a mission church, later described as a chapel-of-ease, on Dale Street. Meanwhile the parish church of St Mary used the same firm to design St George's mission church on the Marsh estate in 1897 and then erected another at the corner of Ridge Lane and Bulk Road the following decade (now the site of the Salvation Army chapel). All of these mission churches, however, were purely functional buildings, shorn of the architectural pretensions of their mother churches; funds were not limitless.

The Roman Catholics benefited from having a wealthy local patroness in the form of the elderly Miss Margaret Coulston, a member of a wealthy family of bankers, curriers and tanners who lived in Skerton. In the 1890s she provided the land and funds to erect St Joseph's at the corner of Aldren's Lane and Slyne Road along with a new presbytery and hall. Designs were drawn up by the national firm of Pugin and Pugin and the church was constructed between 1899 and 1902. The Wesleyan Methodists could also count on the support of prosperous local tradesmen and especially on Norval Helme, wealthy oil cloth manufacturer, town councillor, mayor in 1896 and MP for the town after 1900. They erected a purpose-built hall on the Marsh in 1887 to replace a tiny meeting room in a house in Briery Street, and followed this with a large mission room and Sunday School at the bottom of Westham Street on the Primrose estate the next year.[12] Similar accommodation in

Skerton was provided with a new Sunday School in 1885 and an extension of the Bridge Lane Mission in 1902, again financed by Norval Helme.[13] All of these missions functioned as venues for a variety of other activities such as Band of Hope meetings, bazaars, magic lantern shows, tea parties, improving recitals and talks, and lending libraries, and received generous coverage in the pages of the *Lancaster Guardian* which was owned by E. and J. L. Milner, themselves ardent Wesleyans. The paper also reported in detail the culmination of the Wesleyans' suburban efforts: two impressive chapels in Greaves (1909) and Skerton (1910), the latter essentially the gift of Sir Norval and Mr R. W. Helme.

The major churches, therefore, were relatively successful in colonising the new suburbs, but ultimately they lacked the necessary resources to expand their provision of elementary education sufficiently to cope with the rising numbers of children and the introduction of compulsory schooling. The Wesleyans extended their school on the corner of Sulyard Street and Dalton Square in the 1870s and the 1890s but they made no inroads into the suburbs. After 1902 the premises were handed over to the council which closed them down a decade later and opened a new school on Dallas Road. The Congregationalists had a long-established British School on Aldcliffe Lane, but they, too, failed to maintain initial momentum. The Roman Catholics raised sufficient funds in 1895 to purchase land on Balmoral Road adjacent to the cemetery behind St Peter's, extend their premises, and to open St Joseph's in Skerton the following year, again with the financial assistance of Miss Coulston. The Anglicans, the dominant force in elementary education until the closing decades of the nineteenth century, opened new schools at St Paul's Scotforth in 1879 and St Mary's on St George's Quay two years later and then carried out significant improvements to Christ Church and St Luke's schools during the 1880s. But they lacked the resources necessary to cope with the continually expanding school population in Skerton, Bowerham and on the Marsh in the 1890s. The task of meeting the educational needs of children in these suburbs fell to a new local School Board, established in 1893 and funded from the rates. Plans for new schools at Bowerham and on the Marsh were drawn up and submitted to the council in 1894 and these were followed by new premises in Skerton (1902), Greaves (1906) and on Dallas Road (1912).

Church and board schools, however, catered primarily for workers' children. The sons of the

St Joseph's Roman Catholic School, Aldren's Lane, Skerton, opened in 1896.

local middle class received their formal education at institutions like the Royal Grammar School on East Road and Castle Howell School on Queen's Square, while their sisters were catered for by 'private academies'. Several of these girls' schools were located in the town centre, but they also emerged wherever there were sufficient numbers of potential customers able to pay for their services. The largest and most successful, which appeared in every trade directory between 1881 and 1912 offering boarding and day tuition, was undoubtedly Mrs. J. Paitson's establishment, based in a large property in Regent Street. Others were rather more modest affairs. Miss Agnes Woodhouse ran a boarding school from 46 Rydal Road until the late 1880s and Elizabeth Fisher was listed in 1881 as managing a similar establishment on Bath Street, although she later moved to 2 Dalton Square. Miss Mary Denny and subsequently the Misses K. & A. Greene, joiner's daughters, ran a girls' private school from 28 Borrowdale Road, while on the other side of town Miss Henrietta Liddell operated from premises in West Road in the 1880s and 1890s. The only male proprietor was Robert Satterthwaite whose Higher Grade School was based in premises which he had erected in 1881 at the rear of his terraced house at 20 Ulleswater Road.[14] From the 1900s, however, such schools were superseded by county council provision which culminated in the opening of the girls' grammar school on Regent Street in 1914. Unlike both retailing and church provision, education was by then considered too important to be left to market forces, the unpredictable whim of local benefactors or the uncertain efforts of voluntary associations.

Notes to Chapter Four

1. Centre for North West Regional Studies, University of Lancaster, Oral History Collection, interviews, Mr T.1.L., Mr P.1.L., Mrs M.4.L.
2. Lancaster Borough Building Applications, LRO MBLa acc. 5167, 142, 267 (Ulleswater Road); 1106 (Clarence Street).
3. W. A. Smith, *A History of the Origin and Progress of Lancaster and Skerton Co-operative Society* (1891), and Lancaster and district directories for 1889 (Wells's), 1896, 1899, 1901 (W. J. Cook) and 1912 (Bulmer).
4. For further details on Smith see, M. Winstanley (ed.), *A Traditional Grocer: T. D. Smith's of Lancaster, 1858–1981* (1991).
5. LRO, Building Applications, nos 114, 293, 296, 399, 448, 470, 805, 937, 1010, 1106. The plans described the premises on Williamson Road as a 'public bakehouse'.
6. J. K. Walton, *Fish and Chips and the British Working Class, 1870–1940* (1992), 28–30.
7. *Lancaster Guardian*, 27/8/1892, 1/10/1892.
8. *Lancaster Guardian*, 30/8/1890.
9. *Lancaster Observer*, 1/2/1895, 31/5/1895, 30/9/1895.
10. Unless otherwise stated, details on church and school provision have been gleaned from local directories, newspaper reports and borough building applications deposited at the LRO.
11. P. Andrews, *The Moorlands Testimony* (1980), 2–3.
12. R. Brooke, *100 Years: the Marsh Wesleyan Mission, 1887–1987* (1987), 3–9 (Lancaster Central Library, PT 8925).
13. *Wesley Church, Lancaster: Souvenir of the Centenary Celebration, 1906* (1906), 16–7 (Lancaster Central Library, PT 185).
14. LRO, Building Application, MBLa 457. Details of other private schools have been gleaned from local directories.

Epilogue

The Edwardian Era and After

By the end of the century, Lancaster's inhabitants were housed in very different premises from those of their predecessors even fifty years earlier. Their dwellings were not only more substantial, they were better designed, more effectively lit, and regularly supplied with water. Insanitary middens had been replaced by modern water closets. The streets and estates on which they were located boasted a wide range of residential amenities provided by the local authority, private businesses and voluntary organisations.

An air of optimism also permeated the town. The fortunes of its local industry showed no signs of ebbing; just the contrary. On the outskirts, new dwellings were being erected, the number of home owners was increasing and the demand for rented housing remained buoyant. There seemed little reason to doubt that expansion would continue unabated well into the next century. Councillor William Smith, director of the Lancaster Bank, giving evidence to the Local Board Inquiry held in March 1899 into the extension of the borough's boundaries, stressed the extent of residential development which was then underway. Demand for accommodation in the borough itself was so high that on the Dallas Estate houses were being 'occupied a great deal too soon, before they are really dry'. Most building development was now taking place outside the existing borough boundaries in Scotforth and Skerton, while John Dalton was about to release land in Bulk township for a residential estate. Smith confidently expected 'large building operations to begin there almost immediately'.[1]

These optimistic predictions proved to be wildly wrong. Nationally and locally, the early years of the twentieth century witnessed a dramatic collapse in the property market and a downturn in industrial growth rates. A foretaste of what was in store locally was evident as early as 1902 when the Wagon Works on Caton Road was taken over by a Birmingham firm and its operations scaled down. Although the street plans for Dalton's estate were submitted to the local authority in 1901, the houses were never built. Apart from some substantial terraces on Slyne Road and Myndon Street, building in Skerton virtually stopped. Nevertheless, 175 new dwellings in the town were still completed in 1904, largely in Scotforth and Bowerham to the south and in Ashfield Avenue and Redvers Street off Westbourne Road to the west. By 1907, however, the figure had plummeted to a mere fifty. Dr. Wingate Saul's speculative property development on his Fairfield estate, adjacent to the LNWR railway line, boosted the total dramatically to 271 the following year, but it proved to be financially ruinous. Building there shuddered to a premature halt and the estate was not completed until after the First World War. In 1909 only 33 houses were built in the whole town and by 1911 the figure had dropped to a pre-war low of just twenty. Despite this, the number of unoccupied houses scaled new heights, rising from 428 in 1909, scarcely a good year, to 778 two years later. Some landlords resorted to letting properties rent free in order to protect them from damage.[2] Nevertheless nearly eight per cent of Lancaster's houses were empty in 1911, a figure only surpassed once in the previous century at the height of the Cotton Famine in 1861.[3]

The causes of this dramatic collapse are not difficult to identify. In part the slump was the local manifestation of national downturn in house building brought about by rising interest rates, stagnant living standards and escalating domestic rates. In the late Victorian period the rates burden on property in Lancaster hovered around 3s. to 3s. 6d. in the pound, equivalent to about £1 16s. to £2 2s. per year on a house rated at £12. The expansion of municipal services in the 1900s, especially education, pushed the rate up to 5s. 6d. by 1914, or a hefty £3 6s. per year on a £12 house, equivalent to approximately three weeks' wages for a labourer at the time, or nearly two weeks' income for a skilled craftsman.[4] It is not surprising that the decade leading up to the First World War witnessed the emergence of disgruntled landlords' and ratepayers' associations making vociferous demands that local government expenditure should be cut and the system of taxation reformed.

On top of this, the town's major industries ceased to grow. The expansion of Storey's and Williamson's had been dependent on the buoyancy of the national housing market in the late nineteenth century; in the 1900s they shared in its misery. Waring and Gillows, the high-class furniture manufacturer, also encountered financial problems. The Wagon Works ceased production in 1909. Population, which had risen so dramatically since the 1860s, barely increased between 1901 and 1911 as people left to find work elsewhere. Only the town's service sector, most notably its hospitals, continued to flourish. The town's industrial problems provided a significant disincentive to build houses for letting to the unskilled and semi-skilled manual working class. Builders consequently increasingly placed their hopes in the lower-middle class market, abandoning the construction of the smallest two-bedroomed houses in favour of more substantial terraces with front gardens and bay windows, in the hope that these would appeal to more secure white-collar employees and skilled craftsmen.

During the First World War, domestic house building in Britain virtually ceased. After 1918, despite the promises of 'Homes for Heroes', private developers continued to display little interest in providing working-class accommodation to let, not least because the government retained the rent controls it had introduced during the war. This, and the short-lived economic boom of 1918–21, meant that few individuals wished to become landlords. Private developers consequently returned to putting up houses which they anticipated would appeal to potential owner-occupiers. By the late 1940s the number of houses in Lancaster which were owner-occupied nearly matched those in the hands of private landlords, a marked transformation of the situation prior to 1914.[5] By 1960 they outnumbered them by over three to one, and 90 per cent of the tenanted houses had been built before the First World War.[6] The stagnation and decline of the private rented sector was partially offset by an increase in local authority provision from the 1920s. By then, however, house design, construction methods, and building materials had all been dramatically transformed. The terrace was no longer fashionable. In both the privately-owned and municipal-rented sectors it was displaced by the semi-detached residence. In Lancaster stone was vanquished by brick and pebble dash. A distinctive era in the history of the town's housing had passed.

Notes

1. Local Board Inquiry into the application of the town council to extend the Borough Boundaries, 16 March 1899 (Lancaster Central Library, PT 8572).
2. F.Shaw, 'Report on Houses Let in Lodgings in the City of Lancaster, 1957', Lancaster Borough Council, 1957 (Lancaster Central Library, PT 8177).
3. This figure has been calculated from housing tables in the decennial census.
4. Details of rates can be found in P. J. Gooderson, 'The social and economic history of Lancaster, 1780–1914', unpublished Ph.D. thesis, University of Lancaster, 1974, Appendix 2, 640, extracted from Lancaster Borough Accounts.
5. F. Shaw, 'Report on Housing Conditions for the Public Health Committee of Lancaster City Council', 1948, 12 (Lancaster Central Library, PT 8176).
6. Cullingworth, *Housing in Transition*, 79.

Gazetteer

Lancaster (including Bulk and Scotforth townships)

Dates relate either to the period during which most building plans were submitted to the council for approval, or, when these are not known, to the approximate date by which the majority of the houses are estimated to have been erected. Sources consulted include rate books, trade and street directories, planning applications, newspapers, maps, deeds, surviving properties.

Abbey Terrace, Scotforth (building 1901)
In fact this consists of two separate terraces. Eighteen houses, stone, of 2 storeys with stone ground floor bays, paired doors and small front gardens.

Aberdeen Road, Moorlands (1894–1896)
(south side only) Stone, mostly 2-storey but some of 3 storeys. Built flush with paired doors and a common access to the rear yard between. There is an extra room over this access for every other house. Planning permissions were granted between 1893–1901. Builders included J. Gibson, W. Bibby, A. G. Dowthwaite, C. Dilworth, T. Mawson and Meadowcroft, Till & Holroyd.

Addle Street, Scotforth (c. 1900)
(previously Amos Street)
Brick and render, of 2 storeys built flush with paired doors. A terracotta plaque reads 'D & H 1900', i.e. Dowthwaite & Huntington.

Addlecroft (1898–99)
East side of Scotforth Road between Barton Road and Wakefield Drive. A long terrace in stone, of 2 storeys with stone ground floor bays and small front gardens. The southern part of the terrace has full height bays.

Adelaide Street, St Leonardgate (c. 1879?)
Demolished.

Adelphi Street, Bowerham (1886–88)
Stone, of 2 storeys. Built flush with paired doors. Some houses were added in 1894–5.

Albert Terrace, East Road (before 1864)
Stone, large 3-storey houses with timber ground floor bays. The doorcases have prominent abaci. The 2nd and 3rd house from the east have rounded door heads.

Albion Street, Bulk (1889–90)
Stone, rock-faced, of 2 storeys with dormers and barge-boards. Paired doors. The houses at the east end are larger with front gardens.

Aldcliffe Road (west of Cromwell Road, 1886–88)
Terrace of large stone houses, of 2 storeys and double-fronted. One lower window of each is a bay. Large front garden. Planning permission to Joseph Greene, 1886–88 for 10 houses.

(**Alfred Street**, Greaves
Renamed Charles Street in 1880s.)

Alfred Street, St Leonardgate (before 1881)
South end mostly demolished in 1960s; the last two houses survive within the yard of Heron Chemicals. Stone, of 2 storeys built flush with paired doors and rear extensions. The east side survives: stone of 2 storeys with cellars, built flush with alternating doors and rear access lane.

Alma Road, Greaves (by 1864)
Demolished 1970s to make way for roundabout and road widening in South Road.

Amos Street (renamed Addle Street)

Argyle Street, Moorlands (1893–95)
Stone, of 2 storeys, built flush with paired doors. The north-west corner is occupied by the former Lancaster & Skerton Co-op. dated 1898. Planning permissions were granted for 25 houses in 1893–4

and 1894–5. Builders included W. Wilkinson, W. Bibby, G. Helme, R. Thompson and J. L. Tyson.

Ashbrook Street, Willow Lane (1886)
Stone, of 2 storeys, built flush with paired doors. 6 houses built by J. Johnson.

Ashfield Avenue, Westbourne Road (c. 1901–)
Planning permission was granted in 1901–2 for 21 houses to R. Thompson.

Ash Grove, Greaves (building 1901)
Two separate terraces, to east and west. Stone, of 2 storeys with ground floor bays, the roofs continued over the paired doors as porches. Small front gardens. Planning permission was granted in 1899–1900 for 6 houses to J. Hayton. Building continued after 1901.

Ayr Street, Moorlands (c. 1900)
Stone, with rendered upper storey (over brick?), of 2 storeys with ground floor bays with the roof continued over the paired doors as porches. Decorative barge boards at the eaves. Planning permission was granted in 1898–9 for 2 and 7 houses respectively to W. Bibby and A. G. Dowthwaite.

Balmoral Road, Moorlands (c. 1894–1900)
The upper end is of 2-storey stone houses with houses paired because of the slope. Doors are paired and the roofs of the ground floor timber bays continue over the doors as porches. There are small front gardens. The lower third of the road is similar except that the bays are of stone on the south side and run to full height on the north side. Planning permissions were granted between 1893 and 1897 for a total of 62 houses to A. G. Dowthwaite, J. Johnson and A. Sugden.

Bath Mill Lane, Moor Lane (c. 1837)
Bath Mill Cottages are probably the earliest Victorian houses in Lancaster, dating from 1837. They are still in 'latest Georgian' style. They were built by the Threlfalls of Bath Mill and formed only a tiny part of the projected housing for the mill-workers, cut short by trade depression and the death of John Threlfall. Stone, of 3 storeys with blocked former through passage near the southern end, giving access to the backs, which face on to the canal. The backs are of 3 storeys at the northern end of the row because of the fall of the land. The masonry is 'water-shot'.

Bath Street, Moor Lane
Named after the Bath House, built at its northern end in 1806, which then stood out in the country. It consists of several short terraces of stone 2- and 3-storey houses, plus more recent infill. End terrace (35–39) dates from 1885.

Bay View Terrace, Bowerham (1887)
This row of stone 2-storey houses with paired doors and roofs of the stone ground floor bays continued over the doors as porches occupies the frontage to Bowerham Road between Adelphi St and Golgotha Rd.

Beech St, Willow Lane (1888)
Stone, of 2 storeys built flush with paired doors. The further end of the street is later.

Belle Vue Terrace, Greaves (by 1893)
This row consists of four terraces.

The northern end is the oldest (before 1851) in 'latest Georgian' style, eight houses of 3 storeys with some (added) canted bays. They have long stair windows at the rear. Adjacent to this are four houses of 2 storeys with full height canted bays. Further south come six houses of 2 storeys with canted bays and door hoods on brackets known originally as 'Higher Greaves' and 'Belvidere'. Finally, at the southern end of the row, are eleven houses of 2 storeys with full height canted bays and paired doors. A plaque on this part of the row reads 'Sunny Bank, Greaves, 1891' (q.v.); planning permission for the 3 remaining houses was granted the following year.

In front of the houses runs a roadway raised above the main Greaves Road. It has long been known locally as 'the Monkey Rack' and has an iron railing and access steps leading up from the main road. These seem to be late nineteenth-century additions.

Beresford Terrace, Bowerham (1886))
A terrace of 2-storey paired houses with paired doors and ground floor bays with roofs carried over the doors as porches. There are small front gardens. The terrace occupies the frontage to

Bowerham Road, between Havelock St, and Adelphi St.

Blades Street (1894–1901)
Consists of four half-terraces:
(SW) 2-storey with stone ground-floor bays and paired doors with a shared porch.
(SE) similar but without porches.
(NW) similar to (SW) but with full height bays.
(NE) similar to (SE) but with full height bays.
Planning permissions were granted for a total of 74 houses between 1894 and 1900, all to W. Mashiter. Houses were still being built in 1901.

Bond Street, Moor Lane (by 1881–82)
A cul-de-sac off Parker St, itself a cul-de-sac off Park Road. Stone, rock-faced, of 2 storeys built flush with alternating doors and windows (one pair).

Borrowdale Road, Freehold (1853–92)
Like the rest of the Freehold area Borrowdale Rd is a mixture of individual houses and groups in different styles built over a long period. Its lower end, west of Ulleswater Rd, was built in 1878–79 as matching terraces on both sides. Stone, of 3 storeys with stone dormers. The doors are round-headed and the paired windows at first-floor level are also round-headed. There are timber ground-floor bays and small front gardens.

Boundary Rd, Greaves (1879)
Facing the backs of Railway Street, a row of 12 small houses without rear scullerys, demolished in slum clearance in the 1960s. The site was subsequently used for a roundabout and road-widening in the early 1970s.

Bowerham Terrace, Bowerham (1882)
7 houses, stone, of 2 storeys with timber ground-floor bays. The paired doors have chamfered arches. The terrace fronts on to Bowerham Road, between Dale Street and Prospect Street. Planning permission was granted in 1882 to John Kitchen.

Bradshaw St, Primrose (1883–89)
Stone, of 2 storeys built flush with alternating doors and windows. The first planning permission was granted in 1883 for 12 'cottages' to Thomas Wearing; the majority of the road was built after 1887.

Bridge Road, Greaves (building c. 1901)
Built up on the south side only. The upper houses are of 2 storeys, paired because of the slope, with paired doors and ground floor bays. Small front gardens. The lower house are similar but with full height stone bays and the door hoods carried on brackets. Planning permission was granted for 6 houses in 1900–1 to R. Baines. Jackson Bros were building here in 1901.

Briery St, Lune Road (1877–78)
Stone, of 2 storeys on the east side, built flush with paired doors and through access to yards between. On the west side of 3 storeys with dormers and paired doors.

Brook St, Aldcliffe Rd (1887–90)
Stone, rock faced, on the west side of 2 storeys, with paired doors and stone ground floor bays with roofs continued over doors as porches. On the east side timber ground floor bays; some at the southern end have separate porches.

Brookfield Terrace, Aldcliffe Rd (1879–80)
Fronting on to Aldcliffe Road, between Regent Street and Brook Street, this irregular terrace consists of large 2-storey houses with long front gardens.

Brunton Road, Greaves (north side, 1890; and c. 1901)
Brunton Road, is the upper, northerly part; Brunton Crescent, the lower, southerly part. Brunton Road is, unusually, of yellow brick with full height bays having porches attached. Brunton Crescent has houses of 2 storeys with ground floor bays with roofs continued over the paired doors as porches. Planning permission was granted in 1898–1900 for 23 houses to Mr Lockhart, and Thoms & Sons were building in Brunton Crescent in 1901.

Carr House Lane (1887–89)
A couple of irregular terraces of large houses across the south ends of Dallas Road and Regent Street. One house has '1889' on a lintel over the door.

Cavendish St, Willow Lane (1891–93)
Stone, of 2 storeys, rock-faced with ground-floor bays with roofs continued over the paired doors as porches. On the south side of the street the houses

are similar but have gables over the upper windows. Planning permission was granted in 1891–2 for 19 houses to A. G. Dowthwaite and J. Hartley.

Charles St, Greaves (originally Alfred St) (by 1881)
Only four of the original house are left, the remainder having been demolished in the 1960s for slum clearance and road widening. Stone, built flush, of 2 storeys with alternating doors and windows.

Charnley St, Lune Rd (1876–78)
Named after the Charnley family who owned the land. Since demolition of part of the north side only ends of houses on the south side face the street.

Chatsworth Road, Scotforth (building 1901)

Cheltenham Road, Scotforth (building 1901)

Claremont View, Bowerham (1879)
This terrace fronts Bowerham Road between S Martin's College and Havelock Street. It bears a plaque reading 'Claremont View 1879'. Stone, of 2 storeys with paired doors and timber ground floor bays. There are basements and front gardens. No. 31 was added in 1887.

Clarence St, Primrose (1881–86 and 1891–1901)
There are several terraces in this street reflecting the long time over which it was developed and the variety of builders. 1–33 and 8–20 were built by 1886; the road was extended further up the hill after 1891. At the lower end (west) the south side has 2-storey, flush-built paired houses with paired doors, becoming 3-storey further to the east. On the north side are 3-storey houses with paired doors and stone dormers, like those in parts of Dale St and Prospect St. Further east they have ground floor bays and through access to the yard between paired front doors. The extreme eastern end is of 2-storey houses, not matching. W. Harrison received planning permission in 1901–2 for a further 8 houses.

Clougha View see Golgotha Road.

Coverdale Rd, Willow Lane (1892)
Only the north side of the road is built up. Stone, rock-faced, of 2 storeys with ground-floor bays with roofs continued over the paired doors as porches. Planning permission was granted in 1891–2 for 6 houses to Messrs Whittle & Wilcock and for 18 houses to E. Thompson.

Cromwell Rd, Aldcliffe Rd (by c. 1898)
Stone, of 2 storeys, rock faced. Paired with timber ground-floor bays with roofs continued over the paired doors. There are small front gardens. Planning permission was given in 1894–5 for 18 houses to J. Greene and in 1896–7 for 6 houses to J. Johnson. These represent the east and north-west sides of the current road respectively.

Cumberland View, Bowerham (1886)
This rather curious terrace looks like half an unfinished road. Its access is entirely by rear service alleys from Bowerham Road or Havelock Street. The houses are of 2 storeys, their fronts to long gardens but their backs the main point of access. Brick and render are used instead of stone. Claremont Cottage stands a little to the north, a thin single house which looks like the first of north–south terrace, the rest of which was never built. It looks as though there were several changes to the planned layout here, of which relics survive. Built by William Harrison.

Dale St, Primrose (1881–90)
This street is clearly the work of several builders and represents accretion over some ten years. The different styles of the houses relate to the parcels of land sold off from the Bowerham House Estate. The vendors retained some rights over how the houses would look, which explains the similarity of houses at the south-west end of the street to those in The Grove, just behind, despite the different builders.

Taking the north end first the east side has 3-storey houses with dormers and ground floor bays, the door-heads on brackets. At the middle of the street both sides are of 3 storeys with stone dormers. Houses on the west side have doors like Bowerham Terrace while one house on the east has a lintel dated 1882 over the door. At the south end of the street both sides have full height stone bays and the houses on the west have porches like those in The Grove. This section of the street (40–66) was built by J. Kitchen (Central Library MS 5819 – sale 1888), and seems to have been called Greenwood Terrace in 1889–90. Planning permission was granted in 1882 for 26 houses to Messrs Briggs & Lancaster.

Dallas Rd (1894–1901)
Dallas Rd resulted from the sale to the Corporation of the Dallas Place estate in the 1890s and its subsequent breaking up into units for building. There are at least five divisions within the terrace. From the south the houses are of 3 storeys with dormers and full height stone bays, the porches shared over paired doors. Some have mansard roofs. Further north houses are of 2 storeys. Some have stone ground floor bays with paired doors and hoods on brackets. The most northerly group have full height stone bays. Planning permissions were granted between 1894 and 1901 for groups of 2 to 7 houses to R. Cornthwaite, W. Jackson, R. Baines, F. & R. Wilson and W. Mashiter.

Dalton Rd, Freehold (1869–71)
Only ends of houses face on to this road and were built in conjunction with houses on Grasmere and Windermere Roads.

Davidson St., Moor Lane (1880)
Only the east side was built, permitting a panoramic view to the west over the city from the front windows of those houses. Stone, built flush, of 2 storeys with timber ground floor bays and paired doors.

Denis St, Dry Dock (1872–73)
Stone, built flush, of 2 storeys with paired doors.

Denmark St, Willow Lane (building 1901)
Highly standardised, reflecting the fact that one builder was responsible for all the houses, at least as main contractor. On the north side the houses are of 2 storeys, paired because of the slope, with paired doors and built flush. The south side is the same except for access doors to rear yards between the paired front doors because of the absence of a back street. Planning permission was granted between 1899 and 1901 for 29, 28 and 27 houses to W. Wilkinson (there is obviously some duplication here). *See also* Gerrard St.

Derwent Rd, Freehold (1853–91)
There are no terraces in this part of the Freehold, only single houses and pairs, built over a 40-year period.

De Vitre Cottages, Ashton Road (by 1901)
With Royal Albert Cottages (q.v.) this forms two short contiguous terraces facing the Royal Albert Hospital and clearly both were built to house key workers there. Stone, of 2 storeys with ground-floor bays and small front gardens. Romantic and 'cottagey' in the typical mood of the end of the century.

De Vitre St, Dry Dock (1870–73)
The north side has 2-storey houses with paired doors, built flush. A plaque about the middle reads 'JS RP 1870', commemorating the builders (Shaw & Parkinson). The south side is similar except for ground-floor bays.

Dorrington Rd, Greaves (building 1901)
The longest Victorian terrace in Lancaster. It consists of alternating groups in two styles. All are stone, of 2 storeys with stone ground-floor bays, but some have rear access between paired front doors, while others have a wide passage between with the front door opening off it (cf. Springfield St). Planning permissions for 40 houses were granted in 1900–2 to T. Mawson & Sons, W. J. Edmondson, R. Wilson, Mr Fisher and J. Lockhart. Building went on after 1901.

Dumbarton Rd, Moorlands (1893–1901)
Stone, of 2 storeys with stone or timber ground-floor bays, paired doors and small front gardens. On the east side of the road some houses have full height stone bays and porches. The Moorlands Hotel, at the south end of the road, bears the cypher 'WM 1895' for William Mitchell, the brewer. Planning permissions were granted in

1893–1901 for 24 houses and a shop to R. P. Wilson, W. Bibby, A. G. Dowthwaite and W. Wilkinson. Building was still in progress in 1901.

Dundee St, Moorlands (by 1901)
Stone, of 2 storeys with paired doors, built flush. Planning permissions were given in 1899–1900 for 38 houses to the Moorlands Estate Co. and in 1900–1 for one shop to Till & Holroyd. Building was still in progress in 1901.

Dunkeld St, Moorlands (c. 1901)
Stone, of 2 storeys with paired doors, built flush.

East Rd (below Moorgate) (c. 1896)
Stone, of 3 storeys with ground floor bays and small front gardens. The individual houses of the terrace show a variety of styles. Planning permission was given in 1894–5 for 12 houses to A. G. Dowthwaite.

East Road/Quernmore Road (above Moorgate) see Albert Terrace

Eastham St, Primrose 1889–c. 1895)
The south side is of 2 storeys, built flush with paired doors, the houses themselves built in pairs because of the steep slope. The eastern end of the north side is similar. The western part consists of the ends of Hope St, Bradshaw St, and Langley Road. Planning permission was given in 1891–2 for 6 houses to Charles Dilworth.

Edward St, St Leonardgate (c. 1851–1864)
Demolished in 1960s in slum clearance. It had been built on part of Playhouse Fields (cf. Lodge St, North Alfred St and Seymour St) and the southern end was already built by 1853. A few houses were added in the late 1860s and in 1881.

Elgin St, Moorlands (by1896)
Stone, of 2 storeys built flush with paired doors. Planning permissions were given in 1894–5 for 14 houses to Messrs Bibby, Sugden and Dowthwaite, for 1 shop and 3 houses to E. Holroyd and for 8 houses to S. Waites.

Emerson St, Scotforth (building 1901)
Sixteen houses on the west side, off Addle Street, all built by Dowthwaite and Huntington. Brick, of 2 storeys, built flush with paired doors. Some houses are rendered.

Factory Hill, Bulk
This isolated row of 18 back-to-backs was built for workers at William Jackson's Albion Mill, probably in the 1820s. Workers' housing built by an employer was rare in Lancaster, and this is a particularly early example. It has been totally demolished. While not Victorian in origin, it represented a source of cheap and substandard housing right through the Victorian period and was singled out for particular criticism in Owen's report on the Sanatory Condition of Lancaster.

Fern Bank, Greaves (1878–79 south side)
A cul-de-sac off Greaves Road. Stone, of 3 storeys with dormers and timber ground-floor bays. The round-headed doors each have a pair of round-headed windows over them and there are small front gardens. Houses on the north side were built between 1882 and 1891.

Ford St, Marsh (1875–79)
Only a few houses now face on to the street. Stone, of 2 storeys with paired doors with an access passage to the rear yard in between. In 1867 William Ford owned the land on which this street and its neighbours were built.

Garnett St, Dry Dock (1874–76)
Stone, of 2 storeys built flush, with paired doors.

George St, Penny Street (c. 1844)
All the houses in this street have gone under slum-clearance measures and buildings such as the Police Station and Magistrates' Courts now occupy the sites. A high proportion of Lancaster's early Victorian and substandard back-to- back houses lay along this street. The land was part of Barn Close, sold by G. B. H. Marton of Capernwray to a variety of small builders.

Gerrard St, Willow Lane (by 1901)
Very similar to Denmark St (q.v.) and built at the same time. Stone, of 2 storeys built flush and paired because of the steep slope. On the south side paired doors and a back lane, on the north side access through to yards between paired doors. Planning permissions were given in 1898–9 for 27 houses and in 1899–1900 for 28 houses, both to W. Wilkinson. Building was still in progress in 1901.

Gertrude Place see Park Road

Gladstone Terrace, Bulk Rd (1889–91)
Stone, of 3 storeys with stone dormers and paired doors, rising from a raised stone plinth with a railing along the front, forming the main front access (cf. Moorgate).

Golgotha Rd, Bowerham (north side by 1886–87)
Originally known as 'Clougha View'. Stone, of 2 storeys. On the north side the houses to the west are paired with paired doors and stone ground floor bays with roofs continued over the doors as porches, but those to the east have no porches. Building continued after 1901.

Gordon Terrace, Bowerham Road (1895–96)
This row of stone 2-storey houses occupies the frontage to Bowerham Rd, on the western side, above the Bowerham Hotel. The houses have paired doors, ground-floor bays with roofs continued over the doors as porches, and small front gardens. (known as Gordon Villas in 1901 Directory)

Grasmere Rd, Freehold (1853–86)
As with most of the Freehold Grasmere Road has short terraces within it but no overall building style. About half the houses were built in the 1870s. Nos 1–15 form a terrace set back behind gardens; nos 31–45 are built flush, of 2 storeys with paired doors while 47–57 are similar but for alternating doors. Nos 63–73 have paired doors and small front gardens; just across the road is a similar terrace but for timber ground floor bays. Wash houses were added to 1–15 in 1892.

Green St, Bulk (1889–90)
Stone, of 2 storeys with dormers and paired doors. To the west of Hinde St the houses have access passages to the rear yards between the front doors.

Greenfield St, Moor Lane (1884–85)
Stone, of 2 storeys built flush. On the west side there are paired doors and a rear access lane. On the east there are access passages to rear yards between the front doors because on this side the houses back straight on to those in Melbourne St.

Greenwood Terrace see Dale St

Gregson Rd, Moorlands (1896–1901)
Stone, of 2 storeys built flush with paired doors. Planning permissions were granted in 1896–7 for 4 houses to W. Bibby, in 1897–8 for 27 houses to Moorlands Estate Co. and 14 houses to A. G. Dowthwaite, and in 1900–1 for one shop to R. Booth. This latter was on the corner of Tarbet Street. The Gregson family had lived at the former Moorlands House.

The Grove, Bowerham Rd (1888)
Stone, of 2 storeys with full height stone bays and paired doors under shared porches. There are short front gardens and the houses line the east side only of a private road with gate posts. On the end house is the date 1888. From an agreement in the Central Library (MS 5818) we know that the builder was J. D. Pharaoh. The houses are matched by some at the south end of Dale St, also built on the Bowerham House estate.

Grove St, Greaves (by 1896)
Demolished. This street opened off Brunton Rd opposite the Greaves Hotel behind 'Grove Terrace'.

Grove Terrace, Greaves
The name given to the row of shops, 126–38 in the rate book of 1901–2. This, and Grove Street, were both owned by J. Wildman at the time.

Hala Road, Scotforth (1874)
A stone terrace on the south side divided by a larger, double-fronted house dated 1698. The houses to the west are 2 storeys built flush with paired doors. Nos 2–12 (no. 2 has been demolished) were built as a 'club row', a kind uncommon in Lancaster. A plaque reads 'FUOM 1874' (Friendly United Order of Mechanics). Water closets were added to these houses in 1900. The remaining houses were built by Matthew Hall, gardener, who lived in the older property. Nos 22–26, and a terrace of 6 properties on the north side of the road (now Booth's car park), were built in 1895.

Halcyon Terrace, Lower Greaves (c. 1856)
A short terrace of four houses (nos 52–8) forming two ends and a central pair, all of 3 storeys. The name is lightly engraved into a plaque. At the rear

are long stair windows, an exceptionally late survival of this vernacular tradition.

Hartington St, Moor Lane (1880)
Stone, of 2 storeys built flush with ground floor bays and paired doors.

Hastings Rd, Greaves (building 1901)
Only the north side was built up. Stone, of 2 storeys with stone ground-floor bays and roofs continued over the paired doors as porches. These porches have upright supports carrying 'gothic' tracery. Small front gardens.

Havelock St, Bowerham (1888)
Stone, of 2 storeys built flush with paired doors. North and south sides, built by William Harrison and William Singleton respectively, have slight differences in detail. The corner house (shop) on the north side has a pointed door and a blank plaque. Harrison added a further 3 houses in 1891.

Hawarden Cottages see Hinde St.

Hibbert Terrace, Ashford Rd (c. 1898)
A terrace of seven large seasidy houses now facing Scotforth cemetery. Built for employees of the Royal Albert Asylum.

Hinde St, Bulk (1889–90)
Stone, of 3 storeys with dormers and paired doors. The houses at the north end are slightly lower. At the south end and tucked into a corner are Hawarden Cottages, a pair of similar houses built 1898 by John Laycock.

Hope St, Primrose (1886–89)
Stone, of 3 storeys with stone dormers, built flush. A large block is laid above each door-lintel (cf. Prospect St).

Hubert Place, West Road (1888–93 except 1 & 2, 1877)
Looking for all the world like a seaside promenade terrace, but with no sea. Tall houses of 3 storeys plus a basement. Brick and stone, with bay windows at ground- and first-floor levels. The doors are paired under a flat hood and the dormers have fancy barge boards. Planning permissions were granted in 1892–3 for 4 houses to W. Atkinson and for 3 houses to W. Waites; W. Atkinson had a further permission for one house in 1894–5. The field on which the houses were built was known as West Paddock.

Kensington Rd, Greaves (building 1901)
Stone, of 2 storeys with stone ground-floor bays with roofs continued over the paired doors as porches and small front gardens. On the south side houses have a basic timber trefoil design over the porch. The lower houses on the north side are later. Planning permission was granted in 1900–1 for amended plans for outbuildings to 12 houses to Jackson Bros.

Kirkes Rd, Moorlands (building 1901)
Stone, of 2 storeys, built in pairs. Paired doors, timber ground-floor bays with roofs continued over doors as porches and small front gardens. Planning permission was originally granted in 1896–7 for 32 houses to the Moorlands Estate Co. but this was rescinded the following year when it was found that the proposed road lay on the site of the old Cholera Burial Ground! Permission was given in 1900–1 for 2 houses to Till & Holdroyd and for another 2 houses to W. Bibby. Building was still in progress in 1901.

Langley Rd, Primrose (1889)
Stone, of 2 storeys built flush with paired doors. Only the west side forms a terrace; on the east are the ends of Vincent St, Eastham St, and Clarence St. Thomas Wearing was granted planning permission in 1889.

Laurel Bank, Westbourne Rd (1881)
A single terrace of large houses on a private road off Westbourne Rd. Stone, of 3 storeys with timber ground-floor bays with decorative ironwork, stone dormers and large gardens to both front and rear.

Lily Grove, Greaves (1894–97)
A cul-de-sac off Greaves Road. North side. Large stone houses of 3 storeys with paired doors, full height stone bays and small front gardens. South side. Stone, of 2 storeys with stone ground-floor bays with roofs continued over the paired doors to form porches, and with small front gardens. Baines, Wilson and Shaw are recorded as builders of these houses.

Lindow Square, Queen St (1871–72)
South side. Stone, of 2 storeys with paired doors having square abaci to their heads, timber ground floor bays and round-headed windows. The ends are taller, of 3 storeys. North Side (Lindow Terrace). Similar but plainer and without bay windows. The detached house, 'Wender House', was added in 1875 by Josiah Ball who built the north side of the square.

Livingstone Terrace, Bowerham Rd (by 1901)
Fronts on to Bowerham Rd between Rosebery Ave and Wellington Rd. Stone, of 2 storeys with stone ground-floor bays, paired doors and small front gardens.

Lodge St, St Leonardgate (before 1860)
Now demolished, leaving only one house at the rear of the Grand Theatre. Stone, 2-storey with a projecting drip course. The street was named after Edward Lodge, who had owned Playhouse Fields, the land on which it was laid out. John Lodge Esq. sought the approval of the Board of Health for a new street in 1852 and planning permission for 11 houses was granted 1856–57 so it was almost certainly this one.

Long Marsh Lane (various dates)
There are three short terraces here – five houses (nos 34a–e) are stone, rock-faced, of 2 storeys with paired doors, built flush. The next group (nos 34–26) was originally known as 'Wennington Place' (q.v.) and is similar. The final group is of brick.

Lower Greaves, Greaves (by 1864)
On the west side of Greaves Rd, south of the Pointer roundabout. A terrace to the north of Halcyon Terrace (q.v.). Nos 28–50 are stone, of 2 storeys, plain with a projecting string course and basic triangular lintels/pediments over the doors.

Lune Road, Marsh (1873–75)
Houses were only built on the north side. Stone, of 2 storeys with timber ground-floor bays and small front gardens. There is some variety in the treatment of doorways, with round, pointed and flat doorheads.

Luneside Terrace, New Quay Rd (c. 1895)
A short terrace of houses for Williamsons' workers, some of the very little housing in Lancaster built by the major employers. Stone, of 2 storeys with ground-floor bays with pyramidal roofs. The ends of the terrace have paired doors while the middle has alternate doors. All have small front gardens. Planning permission was granted in 1894–5 for 6 houses to Messrs J. Williamson & Son.

Marsh St, Lune Road (c. 1877)
Two terraces with slight differences. The north side is of reddish stone, 2 storeys built flush with paired doors and entrance to rear yard between. The south side is similar but in lighter stone, rock-faced.

Marton St, Penny Street (c. 1844–45)
Now demolished. The land, like George St part of the former Barn Close, had belonged to G. B. H. Marton of Capernwray and was sold in small plots from 1844.

Meadowside, Bowerham Road (by 1898)
A 'T' shaped cul-de-sac of large houses all of stone and 2 storeys with ground-floor bays, but with a variety of treatments. Those on the west have large romantic front gardens. By 1899 they were lit by electricity, among the first houses in Lancaster to enjoy this amenity. Planning permissions were granted in 1897–8 for 2 houses to W. Nicholson and in 1897–8 for 7 houses to R. Baines. The land formed part of the Bowerham Estate and was developed by its owner, Thomas Barrow.

Meadow St, Willow Lane (1886–88)
Mostly later houses. Only five houses on the right hand side are Victorian. Stone, of 2 storeys, built flush.

Melbourne Rd, Moor Lane (1884–85)
Stone, of 2 storeys, rock-faced with paired doors and shared through access to yards between. Plan-

ning permission was granted in 1882 for the building of 4 streets on the former Woodville Gardens (see Woodville St, Williamson Rd and Greenfield St).

Melrose St, Moorlands (by 1901)
Built up on south side only. Stone, of 2 storeys, built flush with paired doors. The houses are also paired because of the steep slope.

Milking Style Lane, Willow Lane (1887–91)
South side only (north side built after 1910). Stone, of 2 storeys plus dormers, with paired doors and timber ground floor bays with roofs continued over the doors as porches.

Mill St, Dry Dock (1876)
Stone, of 2 storeys built flush with paired doors under shallow porch on brackets. Fifteen of these houses were built by the Lancaster Co-operative Society.

Moorgate, Moor Lane (by 1885)
Terrace below Gregson Institute. Stone, of 3 storeys with paired doors, rising from a raised and railed pavement cf. Gladstone Terrace (see also Woodville Terrace). Planning permission granted to R. P. Moser for 2 dwellings and 10 cottages.

Morningside, Regent Street (by 1881)
A single symmetrical terrace with projecting ends and gardens in front. Stone, of 3 storeys with stone dormers, timber ground floor bays and paired doors.

Newton Terrace, Caton Road (1899)
An terrace isolated from the rest of the town, to the north-east of the former Waggon Works, and developed by the Dalton family of Thurnham. Stone of 2 storeys with paired doors and stone ground floor bays, with roofs carried over the doors as porches. The end house (furthest from town) is of 3 storeys. A plaque reads 'Newton Terrace 1899'.

Nun St, Dry Dock (1876–77)
Stone, of 2 storeys built flush with paired doors. The name seems to originate from the 'Nuns' Fields', as ancient parcel of land originally belonging to St Leonard's Leper Hospital and transferred with it in 1356 to the nuns of Seaton-in-Copeland. After the Dissolution it was sold by the Crown in 1557. Messrs W. Bradshaw, W. Butterworth and G. L. Shaw (builders) signed a covenant in 1876 on land upon which nos 22–26 were subsequently built.

Park Road (originally Quarry Road) Moor Lane (by 1882)
Several terraces, a continuation of Park Square, mostly 1870s. Part of the original Freehold Estate. Nos 35–45 are stone, of 2 storeys with ground-floor bays and small front gardens. No. 47 is of 3 storeys. The even side is of 2 storeys built flush with alternate doors and windows, while 44 and above have paired doors. Above Davidson St, on the left, is 'Gertrude Place' – according to a plaque – four houses of 2 storeys up steps with ground-floor bays, paired doors and small front gardens. On the right (above Parker St) are similar houses but these have shared through access to the yards between the paired doors. Eleven of the houses were built by the Co-operative Society in 1872–3. Planning permission was granted in 1882 for 7 cottages (54–64) to R. Baines.

Park Square, Moor Lane (by 1873)
The lower part is an irregular terrace of 3-storey houses with ground-floor bays and small front gardens. The south-east side of the square is modern. Nos 25–33 are of 2 storeys with timber ground-floor bays and small gardens. Some houses have through access to yards.

Parker St, off Park Road (1881–82)
Only a few houses, each different. Permission to lay out the street was granted in 1881 to H. and J. Hartley.

Parkfield Terrace, Greaves (c. 1856)
Now nos 60–76 Greaves Rd. These form a stone

terrace of nine houses, each of 2 storeys with canted bays. Entrance to no. 76 is in the end elevation of the terrace. The houses were built for W. B. Mortimer and J. Oglethorpe on land which had been known as 'Pointer Field'.

Percy Rd, Greaves (by 1889–90)
South side; stone, of 2 storeys with timber ground floor bays, paired doors and small front gardens. North side; stone, of 2 storeys built flush with paired doors. The rear elevations are in brick. All the houses are built in pairs because of the steep slope.

Perth St, Moorlands (by 1901)
Stone, of 2 storeys built flush with paired doors. The corner house to Aberdeen Road has a brick side wall. Planning permissions were granted in 1897–8 for 28 houses and in 1898–9 for 24 houses, both to the Moorlands Estate Co.

Pickard St, Greaves (1891)
Stone, of 2 storeys built flush with paired doors. West side only; east comprises ends of Brunton Road, Vine Street and Graham Street.

Portland Place (1880–81) Aldcliffe Road
A row of 4 houses built for J. Oglethorpe backing on to Portland Street.

Portland St, Regent St (1876–79 and later in-fill)
A complex development which took some time to build. The east side alone consists of seven different terraces, ranging from 3 storeys with dormers to 2 storeys with ground-floor bays and round-headed windows. On the west side there are two main terraces with timber ground-floor bays, paired doors and small front gardens. Those to the north are larger, those to the south smaller. Planning permission was granted in 1893–4 for 3 houses to J. Beesley.

Portland Terrace, Ashford Road, Scotforth (by 1901)
North side. Building applications for 4 houses in this terrace and for 3 in the short row to the east were submitted in 1896. Stone, of 2 storeys, built flush with paired doors.

Primrose St, Primrose (by 1880–82)
Stone, of 3 storeys with stone dormers, built flush with paired doors. On the north side there are through passages to rear yards between the paired doors. Planning permission was also granted in 1892–3 for 4 houses to Mrs B. E. Lancaster. In 1883 Joseph Lancaster was censured for not building houses here according to the agreed plan.

Princess St, Queen St (c. 1852)
Demolished

Prospect St, Primrose (1881–89)
This consists of several terraces and has two distinct building lines on the west side. West side. From the south, stone, of 2 storeys with paired doors, ground floor bays and small front gardens, then a terrace built flush with paired doors. East side. Stone, of 2 storeys with paired doors, stone ground-floor bays and small front gardens, then 3 storeys, built flush and rock-faced with paired doors and stone dormers. Beyond Clarence St both sides are of 3 storeys but on the west side doors are irregularly spaced. Shops at 96, 98 and 110 were added in the 1890s.

Railway Street, Greaves (1877 south side; 1900–1 north side)
South side: stone, of 2 storeys with paired doors and timber ground floor bays. Planning permission was granted in 1900–1 to Reuben Baines for 6 houses on the north side. North side: stone, of 2 storeys with stone ground-floor bays and paired doors with through access to rear yards between. Alternate houses have an extra bedroom over this passage.

Railway View, Greaves (by 1877)
This terrace, at the rear of Charles St, has been demolished.

Regent St, north of Carr House Lane (1876–85)
This street contains several terraces as well as large semi-detached houses built over a period of about 10 years. West side. 'Lansdowne Villas 1882' (according to a plaque) a large complex group with terracotta-decorated fronts to the gables. 'Hawarden Terrace' with Italianate doors and windows. East side. Stone, of 3 storeys with stone dormers, timber ground-floor bays and paired doors, then stone, of 2 storeys with alternating doors and timber ground floor bays.

67

Regent St, South (1879–86)
East side. Tall, of 3 storeys with dormers and barge-boards. The ground-floor bays have roofs continued over the doors as porches. West side. Elaborate houses of 3 storeys with dormers, ground-floor bays and paired doors.

Ridge St, Bulk (1889–90)
Stone, of 3 storeys with paired doors, quite elaborate on north-east side. The top houses on the north-east side are a conversion of the former Ridge Lane silk mill. There is variety with some dormers and some 2-storey houses on the south side.

Ripley St, Greaves (by 1879)
Planning permission for 8 houses on west side 1879; east side probably earlier. Demolished for road-widening at the Pointer roundabout.

Robert St, Penny St (c. 1850s)
Demolished. This street contained some of Lancaster's few back-to-backs.

Rose Bank, Greaves (1889)
Large houses with front gardens between Lily Grove and Fern Bank. Five houses of stone, 3 storeys with full height stone bays and paired doors. Six further houses are similar except the doors are not paired. Over the latter is a plaque reading 'Rose Bank 1889'.

Rosebery Ave, Bowerham (by 1901)
Stone, of 2 storeys with stone ground-floor bays with roofs continued over the paired doors as porches. Here as elsewhere the effect is of a continuous pentice roof at first floor level, though the houses were built in groups. J. Laycock was granted planning permission for 28 houses at the eastern end of this street in 1897.

Royal Albert Cottages, Ashton Road (by 1901)
Forming, with De Vitre Cottages (q.v.) two adjacent short terraces, built for hospital staff at the Royal Albert Asylum. This terrace is rather more modest. Stone, of 2 storeys with stone dormers and small front gardens.

Rydal Rd, Freehold (1853–90)
Like most of the Freehold Rydal Road is a mixture of various types, including many semi-detached houses built over a long period. There are two short terraces; nos 2–16 are of 2 storeys with stone ground-floor bays and small front gardens. Planning permission for nos 18–32 was granted in 1888. These are larger, still of 2 storeys, with a cellar, full height stone bays with pyramidal caps, paired doors and small front gardens.

St George's Quay (c. 1849–56)
The first terrace on the Quay, nos 1–11, was built following demolition of a preceding terrace in 1849 by the NW Railway, in order to fit in the loop line between Green Ayre and Castle Stations, which runs behind. The terrace was built by a co-operative of a carpenter, two stone-masons and a plasterer, who subsequently divided up the property between them. Stone, of 2 storeys with alternating doors and windows. At the ends and middle through passages give access to the rear and to shared drying grounds at a higher level. There were no rear yards but the privies were placed in two groups, set into the high bank behind the houses. This informal and pre-byelaw terrace is of a type rare in Lancaster.

St Oswald St, Primrose (1888–91)
Houses occupy the north side of the street only, the south side being open to the grounds of S. Martin's College, formerly the military barracks. The terrace is divided into three: on the west (to no. 21) of 3 storeys with 2-storey stone bays and stone dormers, a hipped roof and a small porch; in the centre (to no. 45) of 2 storeys with full height stone bays; on the east similar to those on the west but without a hipped roof. All were built by Simeon Waites and William Mashiter.

St Peter's Road, Moor Lane (by 1881)
Unusually for Lancaster this short terrace of five houses (nos 21–29) is unashamedly of brick. Brick, moreover, in two colours, utilising blue brick dressings. Two storeys, with alternate doors and windows and through access between pairs to rear yards. The ends project slightly further back than the rest. They look just as if someone brought a speculative bargeload of bricks along the nearby canal and decided to build with them then and there, although there is no evidence for this!

Salisbury Rd, Willow Lane (1886–88)
Stone, of 2 storeys built flush with paired doors. Houses at the corners rise to 3 storeys.

Scotforth Rd (by 1883)
An irregular row of 7 cottages to the north-west of the junction with Ashford Road. Building permission for 5 houses (possibly 1–9) was granted in 1881 to G. Webster. A plaque attached to the other two houses reads 'P J & J, 1883'.

Sea View Terrace, Greaves (1893 and 1897)
Terrace of six large irregular stone houses north of Lily Grove. 3 storeys, with full height stone bays and doors under bracketed stone heads or wooden porches. Front gardens. 'Sea View 1893' is inscribed on a stone plaque. The builders of these houses are recorded as Baines, Wilson and Corless.

Seymour St (formerly Moor St.) St Leonardgate (before 1860)
Demolished in 1960s' slum clearance and for road building (the road was never built)

Shaw St, Dry Dock (1871–73)
Stone, of 2 storeys built flush with paired doors. All built by members of the Mawson family.

Spring Bank, South Rd (by 1881)
A short terrace of which six survive (nos 8–18) on the west side of South Road. A centre pediment pulls the group together. A house at the south end of the terrace has been demolished.

Springfield St, South Rd (1873–81)
North side. Stone, of 2 storeys with ground-floor bays and paired round-headed windows at first floor level. There are no front doors as such, the doors being set in wide shared passages between pairs of houses. Small front gardens.
South side. Stone, of 2 storeys with ground floor bays and paired doors, and small front gardens.

Springfield Terrace, South Rd (by 1864)
This row contains several terraces with variations on a theme of 3 storeys and a cellar with short front gardens. Nos 11–19 have round-headed windows, nos 21–29 are plain but with bay windows. Nos 31–37 have Venetian windows, nos 39–41 triple lights, nos 43–45 pointed and nos 47–59 plain. The southern end (nos 59–67) consists of smaller 2 storey houses. Nos 1–9 to the north of Springfield Street were added after 1874.

Stanley Place, Willow Lane (1887–88)
Brick and rough-cast, of 2 storeys built flush with paired doors.

Stirling Rd, Moorlands (by 1896)
North side only, the south side being formed by the ends of Dumbarton Rd, Argyle, Elgin and Dunkeld Streets, and Gregson Rd. Stone, of 2 storeys built flush with paired doors. Because of the steep slope the house are paired also. Planning permissions were given in 1893–4 for a shop and 15 houses to A. G. Dowthwaite and for 4 houses to W. Bibby, who also received permission for a further house in 1894–5.

Sunny Bank, Greaves (1891–92)
Nos 37–55 Greaves Road. Stone, of 2 storeys with full height canted bays, paired doors and front gardens. A plaque reads 'Sunny Bank Greaves, 1891'.

Sydney Terrace, Denis St, Dry Dock (1886)
Stone, of 2 storeys built flush with alternate doors. A plaque reads 'Sydney Terrace 1886'.

Tarbet St, Moorlands (by 1901)
South side only, the north side being formed by backs of houses in Wyresdale Road. Stone, of 2 storeys built flush with paired doors. Because of the steep slope the houses are paired also. Some houses have brick or rendered backs. Planning permission was granted in 1896–7 for all 18 houses to the Moorlands Estate Co.

Thornfield, Ashton Rd (1890–93)
Large stone houses of 2 storeys with stone ground-floor bays, double round-headed windows at first-floor level, paired doors and front gardens. A plaque reads 'Thornfield 1891', but the 1892 O.S.

marks only four houses here, reflecting building in progress.

Ulleswater Rd, Freehold (1853–88)
More developed than the rest of the Freehold by 1870, but still with considerable building activity into the mid-1880s.

(North of Rydal Rd) East side. Stone, of 2 storeys with some ground-floor bays, alternate doors and windows and through access to rear yards. Nos 1–11 are of 3 storeys with stone dormers, ground-floor bays, paired doors and small front gardens. West side. Nos 4–12, 2 storeys with paired doors and small front gardens, nos 26–42, 3 storeys with paired doors and small front gardens, nos 56–94, 2 storeys with paired doors and small front gardens, and nos 96–104, with wide eaves but similar to above.

(South of Rydal Rd) Nos 87–99 are similar but there are some ground-floor bays and over the doors are those triangular lintels (debased pediments?) seen at Lower Greaves (q.v.)

Vicarage Terrace (by 1896)
Stone, of 2 storeys built flush. The two centre houses have paired doors. This short terrace of four houses lies at the foot of Vicarage Lane and above and behind the terrace at the town end of St George's Quay.

Victoria Avenue, Greaves (1901 and later)
North side. Stone, of 2 storeys with stone ground-floor bays with roofs carried over paired doors as porches, and small front gardens. South side (west end only). Stone, of 2 storeys with stone ground-floor bays, paired doors and small front gardens. Planning permission was granted in 1900–1901 for 6 houses to T. & J. Wilkins.

Victoria Terrace, Regent St (by 1890)
Despite its name, this is not a terrace. A plan of 1869 proposes six pairs of houses to be called Victoria Terrace, on the west side of Regent Street, but not all were built.

Vincent St, Primrose (by 1891–93)
Both north and south sides are stone, of 2 storeys built flush with paired doors and built in pairs because of the steep slope. At the north-east end the houses rise to 3 storeys. Planning permissions were granted in 1891–2 for a shop and 18 houses to Simeon Waites, for a shop and 8 houses to W. Mashiter and for 11 houses to F. Wilson, and in 1892–3 for 7 houses to Simeon Waites.

Vine St, Greaves (1890–91)
South side. Stone, of 3 storeys built flush with paired doors. North side. Similar, but of 2 storeys.

Vineyards Terrace, Greaves (by 1871)
Nos 102–106 Greaves Road carry a plaque reading 'Vineyards, West Greaves' but Harrison & Hall's map of 1877 shows the whole group of seven houses (now nos 102–114) under this title. Stone, of 3 storeys with canted bays and pointed dormers. Nos 108–114 have string courses in a contrasting reddish stone probably from the Greaves quarry a little further to the south-east.

Wellington Rd, Bowerham (1898–1901 and later)
Stone, of 2 storeys with stone ground-floor bays with roofs continued over the paired doors as porches. The 1901 Directory records building land and houses building here. Planning permission was given in 1898 for 17 houses to John Laycock and in 1900–01 to various other builders.

Wennington Place, Long Marsh Lane (before 1867)
Shown on a property plan of 1867 these five houses (nos 26–34) are of stone, rock-faced and built flush with paired doors.

West Greaves, Greaves (begun c. 1857)
Nos 116–124 Greaves Road are stone, of 3 storeys with canted bays. Only a few of these houses appear on Harrison & Hall's map of 1877, so clearly the terrace took some time to build. Nos 126–138 (Grove Terrace) seem not to be part of this group. They are of 3 storeys and rock-faced.

The terrace was built on part of a field called 'The Vineyards'.

West Place, West Road (before 1844)
One of the earliest suburban developments in Lancaster this consists, in effect, of two terraces of large houses joined across a wide passage in the middle, giving access to the rear. Stone, ashlar-faced of 3 storeys. Some full height bays seem to have been added to the original façades. Front gardens.

West Road, Marsh (1887–91)
Various houses and shops of mixed styles to the east of the Victoria Hotel (1890–1) and on north side of road.

West Street, Greaves (building 1901)
Only the first twelve houses on the north-east side are of this date. Stone, of 2 storeys with ground floor bays with roofs continued over paired doors as porches. Small front gardens. Planning permissions were given in 1899–1900 for 6 houses each to J. & T. Wilkins and to Mason & Burtholme.

Westbourne Terrrace, Westbourne Road (by 1871)
Nos 2–20 Westbourne Road. Large houses of 3 storeys with canted ground-floor bays and gabled dormers. Round-headed doorcases on brackets. Small front gardens. Only six houses are marked on Harrison & Hall's map of 1877, so the terrace clearly took a while to build.

Westham St, Primrose (by 1888–92)
Stone, of 2 storeys built flush with paired doors. Because of the steep slope the houses are paired also.

Williamson Rd, Moor Lane (1884–85)
Stone, of 2 storeys built flush. Paired doors with through access between to rear yards. The east side is one long terrace, the west side a short terrace to the north, then the ends of Melbourne and Greenfield Streets. Planning permission was granted for building four streets on Woodville Gardens in 1882.

Willow Grove, Quernmore Road (1872)
Stone, of 2 storeys with paired doors. This terrace of four houses was built for employees of the County Asylum (Moor Hospital) but now lies within the curtilege of Nightingale Hall Farm.

Willow Grove, Willow Lane (1886)
A short terrace south-west of Ashbrook Street. Stone, of 3 storeys with stone ground-floor bays, stone dormers, paired doors and small front gardens. A stone plaque is inscribed 'Willow Grove 1886'.

Willow Lane (1886–1891 and later)
There are several terraces fronting the east side of this road. Nos 1–75 received planning permission in 1886; those fronting Coverdale and Cavendish Roads in 1889–91. Stone, of 2 storeys with stone ground-floor bays and paired doors. Planning permission was granted in 1898–99 for 10 houses to W. Wilkinson adjacent to Denmark and Gerrard Street.

Windermere Road, Freehold (1853–89)
Like most of the Freehold this road contains a wide mixture of pairs, threes and fours of houses of a wide variety, all distinguished by large gardens, however small the house. Nos 49–59 are of 2 storeys with ground floor bays, paired doors with steps up, and small front gardens. There is another 2-storey terrace from no. 64 onwards.

Windmill St, Marsh (by 1876–77)
Demolished. The name commemorates the Marsh Mill, which stood at the corner of the street and was demolished in 1880.

Wolseley St, Dry Dock (1876–77)
Stone, of 2 storeys built flush with paired doors. Not all of one build – several have a through passage to the rear yards because of the awkward position backing on to the canal. The Co-operative Society built 13 of the houses here in 1876 (22–34). At the north end of the street is a short cross terrace, not separately named, of 'superior' houses having ground floor bays.

Woodlands Terrace, South Road (by 1896)
Nos 2–6 South Road, on the west side, form a short terrace with door-heads copied from the vernacular.

Woodville St, Moor Lane (1884–85)
Stone, of 2 storeys built flush with through access to rear yards between alternate pairs and alternate

single and paired dormers. Planning permission was granted in 1882 for four streets on the former Woodville Gardens

Woodville Terrace, Moor Lane (1885)
A short uneven terrace fronting Moor Lane below Woodville St carries a plaque reading 'Woodville Terrace 1885'.

Wyresdale Rd (1897–99)
Two short terraces fronting Wyresdale Road, immediately above and below Christ Church, form part of the Moorlands development. Those below Christ Church are stone, of 2 storeys with ground-floor bays having roofs continued over the paired doors as porches and small front gardens. Those above are stone, of 3 storeys with paired doors, porches, dormers, full height stone bays and small front gardens. This group is to a much higher specification than any other part of Moorlands. Planning permission for the houses was granted to Thomas Till between 1897 and 1899.

Skerton

Albert Rd, Lune Street (1879–1881)
Stone, of two storeys with paired doors and ground-floor timber bays, south side only.

Aldren's Lane, Slyne Road (c. 1890–1900)
Several different terraces occupy the south side which was developed over a ten-year period. From the west these are; stone, of 2 storeys with paired doorways, stone ground-floor bays and small front gardens; similar, but with mullioned upper windows and the roofs of the bay windows carried across over the doors as porches (over nos 48/50 is a plaque reading 'Lonsdale Terrace'); similar but slightly taller; at the extreme east a terrace in stone of 2 storeys with dormers, built flush with paired doors and shared passages to the rear yard between. On the north side is one terrace in stone, of 2 storeys with paired doors and small front gardens.

Alexandra Rd (1895–1900)
Long terraces of stone, of 2 storeys built flush with paired doors. Just to the south of Buller Street a small group is of brick, rendered. To the south of Ruskin Road all the houses are of stone, as above, but with mullions to ground floor windows. Gas was supplied to 29 houses here in 1898–9 by Simeon Waites and A. Ireland.

Bank Rd, see Daisy Bank

Beaumont St, Slyne Road (1897–99)
One isolated street at the northern end of Skerton. Stone, of 2 storeys built flush with paired doors and shared access to yards between. Main upper- and ground-floor windows both have mullions. Building still in progress in 1901.

Broadway, Owen Road. (1890–96)
Stone, of 2 storeys built flush with paired doors and mullions to ground-floor windows. At the south-east end houses are of 3 storeys with dormers. At the north-east end houses have chamfers to door and window surrounds. Planning permissions were granted for 48 houses and a shop here between 1891 and 1896 to J. W. Hartley, W. Richardson and J. Wilkinson. Eight of the houses and the shop (80) were for the Lancaster & District Co-operative Society.

Broadway Terrace, Aldren's Lane.
Listed as nos 12–42 in the 1901 street directory.

Buller St, Alexandra Rd (1900)
Confusingly, this street is un-named on the O.S. map of 1913. Buller Street is shown as what is now Central Avenue. North side in stone, of 2 storeys built flush with paired doors. South side similar, but of brick, rendered. All built by Simeon Waites.

Named after Sir Redvers Henry Buller who was Commander-in-chief in South Africa during the Boer War, 1899–1900.

Buller Street, Slyne Road (c. 1901). Now Central Avenue.
A short terrace on the northern side surrounded by later housing. Stone, of 2 storeys with paired doors and stone ground-floor bays. Individual porches, mullioned upper window and small front gardens.

Clarendon Road, off Bank Road (building 1901)
On the east side in stone, of 2 storeys built flush with paired doors. On the west side a terrace of similar houses, but standing on a raised stone plinth, cf. Gladstone Terrace. First planning applications were made in 1898 by John Laycock who built the entire road.

Daisy Bank, Alexandra Road (building 1901) Now Bank Road.
South side, stone, of 2 storeys with paired doors and small front gardens. Houses on the north side are similar but have chamfers to door and window openings and mullions to the ground-floor windows.

Daisy Street, Aldren's Lane (1889–90)
Stone, of 2 storeys with paired doors and small front gardens.

Derby Road (1879–82)
At the west end; stone, of 2 storeys with paired doors and small front gardens; this seems to have been known originally as 'Lune Terrace'. To the east of Albert Road; stone, of 2 storeys and cellars with timber ground floor bays, paired doors and small front gardens. This terrace has a prominent corbel table supporting the gutter, similar to many other terraces in Skerton. George Turner built many of these houses.

Earl Street (1878–81)
Stone, of 2 storeys built flush with paired doors, of more than one build. No. 29 is a former shop in the middle of the row, and there are former shops at the south west and north west corners. 39–45 were built by J. W. and S. Waites, stonemasons; no. 10 is the first house to be built by Amos Dowthwaite.

Edith Street, Slyne Road. (1892–1900). Now known as Vale Road.
The eastern end of the road only has houses on the north side. Stone, of 2 storeys with paired doors, stone full-height bays and small front gardens. Further west, on both sides, stone, of 2 storeys with paired doors stone ground-floor bays, mullioned upper windows and small front gardens. The bays and porches are covered by a continuous outshut of slate, carried on timber posts. Similar houses line both sides of Slyne Road immediately to the north. Street layout granted 1892 to Charles Edward Whalley of Richmond house. A. Dickinson was still building houses in 1901.

Gardner (or **Gardener**) **Road**, Aldren's Lane (by 1901)
Stone, of 2 storeys built flush with paired doors. Ground-floor windows have mullions. Some houses on the north side have shared passages to the rear yard between the front doors, because of the awkwardly constricted site. Planning permissions were granted in 1897–8 for 12 houses to Simeon Waites and for 8 houses to J. Musgrave, and in 1898–9 for 4 houses to J. Wilkinson.

Halton Road, north of Ruskin Road (1889–94)
Short mixed terrace of 2- and 3-storey stone dwellings with front gardens. 39 & 41 have plaques: 'Ivy Cott 1892' and 'Holly Cott 1892'.

Ivy Terrace, Halton Road (1898)
Stone, of 2 storeys, with porches, ground floor bays and front gardens. Plaque reads 'Ivy Terrace, Lune Bank C & P 1899'. Patterson was an auctioneer and accountant who lived on Pinfold Lane.

Lord Street, Lune Street (by 1889)
Stone, of 2 storeys built flush with paired doors, which have corniced lintels over them. Some houses were built by R. L. Dilworth.

Lune Street (1878–80)
This long street is in several segments. From the west these are; stone, of 2 storeys with paired doors and stone or timber ground-floor bays; (either side of Albert Road) stone, of 3 storeys with ground-floor bays and dormers; nos 69–59, stone, of 2 storeys like those at the west end; nos 57–17, stone, of 3 storeys, like those near Albert Rd. On the end of no. 17 is a faintly inscribed stone

reading 'Westbourne Terrace'. No. 51 (formerly 18 Westbourne Terrace) was described as 'lately built' in 1882. Planning permission was given for an additional 2 houses in 1891–2 to Messrs J. & C. Fell.

Lune Terrace (by 1884)
The old name for the south-west end of Derby Road (q.v.).

Myndon Street, Slyne Road (building 1901)
A cul-de-sac off Oxford Street of 22 stone, 2 storey houses with ground-floor bays and small front gardens. Six houses were listed in the 1901–2 rate book.

Norfolk Street, Owen Road (1891–94)
Stone, of 2 storeys built flush with paired doors. On the south side and at the east end of the north side houses have a central mullion to ground-floor windows. Planning permission for an additional 2 houses was granted to R. Taylor in 1899–1900.

Olive Road, Aldren's Lane (by 1901)
Stone, of 2 storeys built flush with paired doors and mullions to ground-floor windows. Planning permissions were granted in 1897–8 for 14 houses to Mr J. Thompson and others, in 1898–9 for 10 houses to Mr J. Thompson, and in 1899–1900 for 28 houses to J. Wilkinson. Gas was supplied to 14 houses here in 1898–9 by E. Thompson.

Owen Road (1889)
Four houses and two shops, stone, 3 storeys, with bays to first two floors, paired doors and porches, between Norfolk Street and Pinfold Lane. The shops' entrances were initially on the adjoining streets and were numbered as such.

Oxford Street, Slyne Road (1897–98)
A short terrace of large stone houses, of 2 storeys with paired doors and porches, full height stone bays and small front gardens.

Pinfold Lane, Owen Road (by c. 1889)
On the north side stone, of 3 storeys with alternate doors and windows, stone ground floor bays, dormers and small front gardens. The roofs to the bays and the porches take the form of a continuous outshut. At the eastern end smaller 2-storey houses relate more to the development of burgage plots on Main Street than to Pinfold lane itself (these may represent Victoria Terrace). At the west end of the south side are a few stone houses of 2 storeys with paired doors, stone ground floor bays and small front gardens. Further east the buildings are more recent.

Regent Road, Alexandra Road (1899–1900). Now Ruskin Road.
On the north side stone, of 2 storeys built flush with paired doors. On the south side similar, but ground-floor windows have mullions. Built by Waites and Laycock.

Ruskin Road see Regent Road

Slyne Road (from 1893)
37–45 Edith Terrace (west side) and 46–54 were built first in 1893–94 by R. Thompson and J. Hartley. Stone, of 2 storeys, mullioned upper windows, porches. Building applications for 9–35, a mixed terrace on the west side were submitted 1894–97. Stone, 2-storey houses with bays, some with porches. G. Turner was building at the far east end between Beaumont Street and Central Avenue in 1901. These are 2 storey, with bays, porches, mullions to upper windows and front gardens. Other houses on the road are after 1901.

Vale Road see Edith Street

Victoria Terrace (by 1886) see Pinfold Lane

Westbourne Terrace see Lune Street

Primary Sources and Select Bibliography

Much of our evidence for these houses still survives physically. We can survey and analyse the standing buildings, which in a surprisingly large number of cases have not been substantially altered since they were built. This gives us the building plans, but also some indication of the uses to which space was put. Where alterations have taken place it is usually to provide more space for each individual and to provide more luxurious services. This can mean that bedrooms are sacrificed to bathrooms, wash-houses to kitchens and yards to garages.

Direct evidence for the history of individual houses can sometimes be gained from deeds, although these vary in quality and survive (or are accessible) patchily. In particular early deeds may have been lost, destroyed, or exist only in epitome. Lancaster City Council has a very large number of deeds, relating to its roles as property owner and acquirer by compulsory purchase of land or houses for road-building etc. This collection of deeds includes many for properties now demolished, though these can still be of interest since they often represent the earlier, pre bye-law houses and dwellings in yards and courts.

Planning permissions are recorded from the 1880s onwards in Corporation Minutes, while the applications themselves are deposited in the Lancashire Record Office at Preston. Some of these include very detailed drawings and layouts.

From trade directories we can pick up the names of new streets and sometimes of the terraces within them, within perhaps no more than five years of building. This source also indicates the social standing of the new street, at least initially, by virtue of the occupations listed there. Some caution needs to be used. Directories often omit new information or repeat outdated information. They cannot offer a date from which a street was begun, but can show the point at which people moved in. Many directory entries of the late nineteenth century show terraces where people are already living at one end while the middle is as yet unoccupied and the far end is 'building ground'. Clearly at times the pressure for housing led people to move in while the plaster was still wet.

Some groups of people are invisible to such directories. Even the poorest areas tended to have a few shops, but some streets will have been omitted from the directory because they had no interest from a trade point of view, not because they were uninhabited. The great majority of yards and courts do not figure, since any shops tended to be on the street frontage, not in the yard. The most useful directories we have found are those such as Wells' or Cook's, dating from the very end of the century. These include street directories listing and locating every house, in addition to lists of those businesses which chose to advertise.

Rate-books are of the utmost use, since they indicate ownership of property, relative values and exactly what was in existence at the time. They can also be used comparatively, year against year. The surviving rate-books are to be found in the Lancashire Record Office. Others have trodden parts of this way before, including Geoffrey Boulton in his unpublished 1976 University of Liverpool MA thesis, 'Lancaster 1801–1881, a geographical study of a town in transition'.

Maps are potentially very useful, but they should be used with caution. Maps are usually out of date by the time they are printed. The larger the scale, the more out-of-date. Lancaster has good coverage in O.S. 6″ and 60″ maps of the 1840s, Harrison & Hall's map of 1877, the O.S. 1:500 scale of 1892 (particularly good because of its huge scale) and O.S. 25″ maps of 1913 and onwards. There are crucial gaps, covering the great changes which occurred between 1877 and 1892, or at the turn of the century. Some original layout plans survive, such as those for Moorlands (1893), the Freehold (1852) and Dry Dock (c. 1880), while a few are to be found in deed parcels, especially when the site was complex or ownership hinged on the original conveyance of a block of land.

Select Bibliography

J. Burnett, *A Social History of Housing, 1815–1970* (1978).

E. W. Cooney, 'The Origins of the Victorian Master Builders', *Economic History Review*, 8 (1955), 167–76.

J. B. Cullingworth, *Housing in Transition: a case study of the City of Lancaster, 1958–62* (1963).

M. J. Daunton, *House and Home in the Victorian City: Working-Class Housing 1850–1914* (1983).

M. J. Daunton, 'Housing' in F. M. L. Thompson (ed.), *The Cambridge Social History of Britain*, vol. III (1990), 195–250.

H. J. Dyos, *Victorian Suburb: a study of the growth of Camberwell* (1961).

D. Englander, *Landlord and Tenant in Urban Britain, 1838–1918* (1983).

S. M. Gaskell, *Building Control: National Legislation and the Introduction of Local Bye-Laws in Victorian England* (1983).

J. P. Lewis, *Building Cycles and Britain's Growth* (1965).

S. Muthesius, *The English Terraced House* (1982).

A. Offer, *Property and Politics 1870–1914: Landownership, Land, Ideology and Urban Development in England* (1981).

C. G. Powell, *An Economic History of the British Building Industry, 1815–1979* (1980).

E. Roberts, 'Working-class housing in Barrow and Lancaster, 1880–1930', *Trans. Lancs. & Ches. Historic Society*, 127 (1977), 109–31.

E. Roberts, *Working-Class Barrow and Lancaster 1890 to 1930* (1976).

R. G. Rodger, *Housing in Urban Britain, 1780–1914* (1995).

S. B. Saul, 'Housebuilding in England 1890–1914', *Economic Hist. Review*, 15 (1962), 119–37.

F. M. L. Thompson, *The Rise of Respectable Society: A Social History of Victorian Britain, 1830–1900* (1988).

A. White (ed.), *A History of Lancaster 1193–1993* (1993).

B. Trescatheric, *How Barrow Was Built* (1985).

J. W. R. Whitehand, 'The Makers of British Towns: architects, builders and property owners, c. 1850–1939', *J. Hist. Geog.*, 18 (1992), 417–38.